Developing Teaching and Learning in Higher Education

Higher education is facing increasing demands for teaching excellence and as a result new lecturers are now expected to have training and induction in teaching and learning strategies. This book provides new lecturers with an easy and accessible guide to planning and preparing teaching sessions, teaching a diverse student population and assessing students' progress and achievement. Furthermore, the book recognises the demands of the Institute for Learning and Teaching (ILT) and guides the lecturer through the process of reflection and development required to become a member of the ILT.

The book addresses key areas, as recommended by the ILT, including:

- planning and preparation;
- conducting teaching and learning sessions;
- assessment and evaluation;
- revising and improving teaching;
- leadership, management and administration;
- continual professional development.

This accessible, user-friendly book is directly related to most induction programmes which new lecturers attend. It is essential reading for all new and established lecturers, and academics keen to develop their teaching and learning strategies.

Gill Nicholls is Professor of Education and Director of the Institute for Learning and Teaching at King's College, the University of London.

Developing Teaching and Learning in Higher Education

Gill Nicholls

London and New York

First published 2002 by RoutledgeFalmer
11 New Fetter Lane, London EC4P 4EE

Simultaneously published in the USA and Canada
by RoutledgeFalmer
29 West 35th Street, New York, NY 10001

RoutledgeFalmer is an imprint of the Taylor & Francis Group

© 2002 Gill Nicholls

Typeset in Sabon by RefineCatch Limited, Bungay, Suffolk
Printed and bound in Great Britain by
The University Press, Cambridge, United Kingdom

British Library Cataloguing in Publication Data
A catalogue record for this book is available from the British Library

Library of Congress Cataloging in Publication Data
Nicholls, Gill.
    Developing teaching and learning in higher education /
    Gill Nicholls.
        p.   cm.
    Includes bibliographical references and index.
    1. College teaching – Great Britain.   2. Learning.   I. Title.
LB2331 .N53 2002
378.1′25—dc21   2001034870

ISBN 0–415–23696–7 (paperback)
ISBN 0–415–23695–9 (hardback)

Contents

Illustrations

Figures

Tables

Acknowledgements

I would like to thank Anna Clarkson of Taylor & Francis for the opportunity to write this book and for all the support given throughout the development.

The book is a product of many conversations and teaching sessions with fellow academics and new lecturers. I am indebted to them all for the endless encouragement to complete the book.

Special thanks go to my colleagues at the Institute of Education for their help with the portfolio of evidence and King's College where the book was completed.

Chapter 1

The changing context of teaching and learning in higher education

Introduction

The increasing demands for teaching excellence in higher education have led to new academics needing induction into what it is to teach and how students learn. In the United Kingdom in particular, the creation of the Institute for Learning and Teaching (ILT) has increased the pressure on universities to provide and deliver courses that meet the demands and recommendations of the ILT within the domain of teaching and learning.

This book recognises the demands of the ILT, but also demonstrates that teaching and learning require a positive approach, one that encourages diversity, creativity, enthusiasm and commitment to the art of teaching. It also suggests that the individual approach to professional development within the context of teaching and learning is essential if effective learning environments are to be created and sustained. The book recognises and encourages the way in which teaching is understood and pedagogical relationships practised, and that these are different across subject areas.

Underpinning this book is the recognition that ILT membership is advisable for new and established academics alike. However, new academics will require help in a different way from established academics, part of which is an appreciation that teaching is a fundamental way of learning their subject and that it is closely linked to research and scholarship. The key elements to achieve membership are for all academics to demonstrate:

1   Knowledge of their subject and its pedagogy;
2   Practice that is underpinned by a range of professional values.

In order to help new academics, existing lecturers and planners of courses achieve these goals, this book has been constructed in such a way as to facilitate learning and development. The design is progressive in approach, with diagrams, tasks, and points for consideration and exemplars to assist development.

The book addresses six basic generic issues as recommended by the ILT. These are:

1   Planning and preparation;
2   Conducting teaching and learning sessions;
3   Assessment and evaluation;
4   Reviewing and improving teaching;
5   Academic administration, management and leadership teaching;
6   Continual professional development.

Within each of the identified areas, tasks and points for consideration are given to help the new academic deal with complexities of developing teaching and learning in higher education. Although the six areas of the ILT guide the framework of the text, the book takes a more in-depth view of teaching and learning. The perspective given is one that aims to help the new academic understand the reasons for engaging in some of the activities such as planning and preparation that are key to successful and effective teaching and learning. The ILT expects academics to collect evidence and through this evidence to illustrate development within the six categories by showing they have knowledge and understanding of underpinning knowledge associated with their subject. These include:

- the subject material that they will teach to their students;
- how their subject is learned and taught;
- how students learn, both generically and in their own subject;
- teaching approaches;
- the use of learning technologies;
- techniques for monitoring and evaluating their own teaching;
- their institution's mission and how it affects teaching and learning strategies;
- implications of quality assurance for practice;
- regulations, policies and practices affecting their own work;
- the professional values underpinning practice.

The main aim of this book is to provide new academic staff with the opportunity to reflect upon their teaching and academic experiences in a way that enhances and possibly changes their teaching and learning environments within their academic practice. It suggests and thus focuses on teaching, learning and academic practice as a complementary set of ideals, aspirations or outcomes that include student learning outcomes and the advancement of knowledge. The book takes each element identified by the ILT but tries to link and make connections between the various components and the implications and consequences each component may have on the other. Thus the book integrates theory and practice in a pragmatic and helpful way. Throughout the book there are stopping points, entitled 'points for consideration'; these have been placed strategically to assist and enhance reflection on teaching, learning and academic practice.

In order to understand why teaching and learning now takes such a prevalent place in higher education debates it is necessary to examine, albeit briefly, the history and inception of the Institute for Learning and Teaching.

Brief history of the Institute for Learning and Teaching (ILT)

> University teaching might be called the hidden profession. It is practised as a secret rite behind closed doors and is not mentioned in polite academic society.
>
> (Mathews, quoted in Layton, 1963, p. 8)

Prior to the Dearing Report (NCIHE, 1997), it might have been possible to support this view of teaching in many British universities, a view that assumed teaching skills to be conferred on lecturers as a postgraduate gift that was neither appropriate nor necessary to enquire into or closely scrutinise. Communication of knowledge was considered secondary to its advancement, the balance between teaching and research being heavily biased towards the latter. However, Dearing challenged this perspective by stating that:

> Institutions and their staff face a great challenge if our vision that the United Kingdom should be at the fore front of world practice in learning and teaching in higher education is to be realised.
>
> (Paragraph 8.56)

Demands of the ILT

These have changed and continue to change as this book is being written, and for this reason it is necessary to explore what the demands were, how they have changed, what they are now, and what they may be in the future. The demands will, and already have had, implications for those involved in teaching and learning in the higher education community.

Early requirements and recommendations

The proposed functions of the ILT following the Dearing Report had three main purposes:

1   The accreditation of programmes of training for higher education teachers;

2   The research and development in teaching and learning;
3   The stimulation of innovation.

This proposed approach is intended to provide a framework around which individual institutions (or consortia) can plan and develop their own pathways and programmes.

Levels of membership

Within the national framework the proposed structure was to have three levels of membership: associate member, member and fellow. The criteria for higher levels of membership are show in Table 1.1. The criteria focus on mainstream teaching and learning activities that have been broadened to include activities carried out by other staff in support of teaching and learning. The specified requirements for ILT membership are explained in terms of a range of teaching outcomes that include knowledge, understanding and a range of skills and values a teacher acquires through training and/or experience. The categories of membership are distinguished by the range of outcomes achieved by individuals and their level of professional autonomy and responsibility.

Table 1.1 Booth membership framework

Category or level of membership	Illustrative range of responsibility
Associate Part 1	Classroom practice, marking, evaluation of teaching
Associate Part 2	In addition to above: Design of a module, unit or series of teaching sessions, design of assessment, evaluation of modules
Member	In addition to the above: Curriculum/programme design (e.g. across a degree), improvement of curricular/programmes, innovation in own course practice, evaluation of programmes, supervision of associates
Fellow	In addition to the above: Leader of change (across institutions or disciplines) in teaching or curricula, through research, publications, work on disciplinary or professional bodies

Five broad areas of responsibility associated with higher education (HE) teaching have been identified, and members are expected to achieve all or most of the outcomes linked under the five broad headings. These are:

1   Planning and preparation;
2   Conducting teaching and learning sessions;

3   Assessment and evaluation;
4   Reviewing and improving teaching;
5   Academic administration, management and leadership teaching.

Continual professional development is the sixth element that all academics must be actively involved in.

Routes to membership

The ILT, having been set up as a professional body for higher education staff involved in teaching and the support of learning, is envisaged in time as being the main source of professional recognition for those engaged in teaching and learning support in higher education.

As a member of this professional institution a member would be able to:

- obtain recognition for the professionalism of their teaching;
- keep updated on developments in teaching and learning in HE and on methods of self-evaluation and improvement;
- obtain information and guidance on implementing new learning and teaching strategies, including information communication technology (ICT);
- have access to new research, publications and conference seminars.

The proposed routes to membership and the criteria by which routes are identified have the following key features that are based on five areas of professional activity:

1   Teaching and/or supporting learning in HE;
2   Contribution to the design and planning of learning activities and/or programmes of study;
3   Provision of feedback and assessment of students' learning;
4   Contribution to the development of effective learning environments and student support systems;
5   Reflection on personal practice in teaching and learning and work to improve the teaching process.

Within these five professional areas it is also stated that:

- Initial membership routes would be designed to recognise and reflect the current expertise of experienced staff.
- That there would be both individual and institutionally based routes that reflect the diversity of educational contexts within the sector which individuals will be able to apply for membership directly to the ILT, rather than through an institution, if they so wish.

- The membership criteria will be informed by underpinning knowledge and professional values including commitments to learning and scholarship as an integral part of teaching.

In Appendix 1 of the ILT's document on accreditation it is stated that:

Courses seeking accreditation should be designed with an awareness of the core knowledge and professional values that are expected of members of the Institute for Learning and Teaching in Higher Education.

Consideration of the core knowledge and values is a means to understanding the nature and context of teaching development that the ILT will be looking for.

Core knowledge

Members of the ILT will be expected to have knowledge and understanding of:

- the subject material they will be teaching;
- appropriate methods for teaching and learning in the subject area and at the level of the academic programme;
- models of how students learn, both generically and in their subject;
- the use of learning technologies appropriate to the context in which they teach;
- methods for monitoring and evaluating their own teaching;
- the implications of quality assurance for practice.

Professional values

Members of the ILT will be expected to adhere to the following professional values:

- a commitment to scholarship in teaching, both generally and within their own discipline;
- respect for individual learners and for their development and empowerment;
- a commitment to the development of learning communities, including students, teachers and all those engaged in learning support;
- a commitment to encouraging participation in higher education and to equality of educational opportunity;
- a commitment to continued reflection and evaluation and consequent improvement of their own practice.

The core knowledge and values are clearly described and laid down by the ILT. This book attempts to cover all the areas specified by the ILT. However, the book goes beyond these basic requirements. It suggests ideas and alternatives for the new academic practitioner to engage with, both in the context of institutional development, but most importantly personal development.

Using the book to its best advantage

The book is structured so that the elements of appropriate theory are incorporated and often introduce each element of learning and teaching in higher education. The theory is interwoven with points for consideration designed to help you identify key features that relate to behaviour or issues. A variety of methodologies are used to help you generate evidence of teaching, learning and academic practice (e.g. reflecting on elements of course design and development, observation of other lecturers' teaching, student evaluations and your own planning and preparation techniques).

The nature of the evidence collected is aimed at generating your portfolio of evidence for accreditation. This portfolio will be a personal record of teaching, learning and academic practice. It will represent your development in the areas of teaching and learning and demonstrate areas of competence and areas for future development. The evidence identified is collected throughout your programme and should show a developmental approach.

The book is designed to be used in a number of ways. It can be dipped in and out of as a means of a reference point to help with a specific problem, question or issue that you may need to consider and to help you reflect on a problem or issue encountered in a teaching/learning scenario.

Finally, the book attempts to transmit the professional elements that are required by a teacher in higher education. The need to understand and interpret professional knowledge, professional judgements and discipline knowledge are all tackled. It emphasises that in order to become effective, teaching needs to be seen as a continuous creative and problem-solving activity. Each student group is different, as is each individual within that group. Each student and each group of students will have their own identities, learning styles and approaches to learning. Planning and preparing teaching and learning environments that complement such diversity are a constant challenge to the teacher in higher education. This book attempts to make that challenge less stressful and more achievable.

Chapter 2

Developing teaching and learning

Introduction

The expectations of ILT membership are clear: lecturers have to demonstrate competence in teaching and learning in a variety of contexts, thus gaining membership. This is the baseline from which many courses that aim at developing teaching and learning skills start; however, there is more to effective teaching and learning than simply gaining membership to the ILT. What does it mean to develop teaching and learning skills? Addressing this fundamental question requires an understanding of the teaching role as well as of student learning and the contexts in which these occur. The lecturer's responsibility is to ensure that students learn. Teaching is a very personal activity and while certain teaching styles and strategies may suit one teacher they might be totally inappropriate for another. There is no one way to teach, provided students learn a variety of approaches and strategies that may be used. Teaching styles will vary from group to group and from individual to individual. Teaching is a continuous activity that requires creative thinking and problem solving. Effective teaching requires:

- the lecturer to transform his or her knowledge of the subject into suitable tasks, which lead to learning;
- the learning experience structured by the lecturer to match the needs of the learner;
- a balancing of the students' chances of success against the difficulty required to challenge them;
- an understanding of the complex interrelationships of a whole range of factors, the most important of which is the way students learn.

The teaching role of the lecturer

The lecturer's role is diverse and challenging: not only will you be expected to research, gain grants, prepare academic papers and contribute to scholarship, but to teach and develop the curriculum. The role of teacher will require the lecturer to be involved in:

- subject teaching;
- session planning;
- setting and marking of assignments;
- assessing student progress in a variety of ways including marking end-of-module assignments and examination papers;
- writing reports for a variety of audiences including exam boards and external examiners;
- recording student achievement;
- working as part of a subject team;
- curriculum development and planning;
- undertaking visits and field courses where appropriate;
- feedback to students;
- evaluating the programme and your teaching.

What makes an effective teacher?

Throughout this book teaching is considered alongside student learning; however, it is necessary to consider what attributes constitute effective teaching and thus try to assimilate them in a way that helps student learning. Table 2.1 shows the attributes that effective teachers are said to have, although all attributes are not expected to be found in all teachers. These attributes are dependent on an individual, but they do demonstrate the

Table 2.1 Attributes of effective teachers

Personal attributes	Professional attributes	Professional skills
Humorous	Organised	Makes work relevant
Relaxed	Flexible	Actively assists students to learn
Imaginative	Well prepared	Uses a variety of teaching methods
Accessible	Articulate	High expectations
Listens	Up to date in subject knowledge	Explains clearly
Fair	Subject expert	Gives praise
Friendly	Good time-keeping	Demonstrates fairness and equity
Supportive		
Enthusiastic		

elements that a good, effective teacher needs to develop. Alongside these attributes is the notion of teaching style.

What does teaching style mean?

Teaching style is the term used to describe the way a learning experience is conducted. It is derived from the behaviour of the teacher and the strategy chosen for learning to take place.

Lecturer behaviour means the way the lecturer conducts him- or herself during the teaching session; this involves the way the lecturer relates to the students. They may be aloof or distant from the students, or they may be enthusiastic and friendly. The lecturer indicates their expectations to the students through their behaviour when conducting a teaching session.

Teaching strategy refers to the choice and range of teaching methods used for a teaching session; this may include group work, problem solving, discussion or practical work. In any teaching session it is important to use a range of strategies to keep the students motivated and interested. Teaching style is difficult to pinpoint. Teaching styles are usually associated with a particular approach such as experiential, didactic, teacher directed, student centred, theoretical, traditional, transmission, content based, processed based and facilitative. These descriptions give an indication of the nature and context in which a lecturer might approach student learning. Usually, teaching styles are chosen to suit the characteristics of the student body as well as the preferred teaching style of the lecturer.

Teaching style and learning outcomes

Effective teaching and learning requires flexibility by the lecturer, and this in turn necessitates the use of a variety of styles. The teaching style adopted should best suit the objectives and learning outcomes stated for the particular session. (Learning outcomes and programme aims, objectives and learning outcomes are discussed in detail in chapters 3, 4 and 5.) If a lecturer uses a particular teaching style all of the time there is a danger that students will not achieve the learning outcomes of the programme.

Choosing a teaching style

Teaching style in essence is a personal choice; however, there are several issues that need to be taken into consideration prior to planning a teaching session. These include:

- characteristics of student body;
- size of student group;
- learning outcomes;

- nature of knowledge to be taught;
- professional knowledge;
- extent of lecturer's pedagogic knowledge;
- environment in which teaching is to take place;
- personal preferences.

As mentioned above, choice of teaching style is affected by a variety of issues, but one of the most significant is that of personal beliefs, views and assumptions about teaching and learning, as well as one's professional knowledge. Trigwell and Prosser (1990) show how personal theories of teaching and learning affect the way academics engage with the process of teaching, and the activities they choose to transmit this information. For example, lecturers hold differing views in relation to asking students questions during a lecture, the role that group work has in the development of student thinking and the place of discussion within a teaching session. Decisions made about the balance of activities and alternative teaching approaches within a teaching session influence not only the style the lecturer adopts but also the balance between the process of learning and the teaching that takes place.

What constitutes a teaching style?

Teaching style falls into three basic categories (Barnes, 1987): that of closed teaching, framed teaching and negotiated teaching.

- *Closed teaching*: In this approach the lecturer is considered to be didactic and formal in his or her teaching, there will be little involvement by the students, and generally material and information is given rather than discussed or shared.
- *Framed teaching*: In this approach the lecturer is considered to provide a structure for the teaching session within which the students are able to contribute their own ideas, views and interpretations to the information being given.
- *Negotiated teaching*: In this approach the lecturer is considered to provide a teaching session where the direction of the session has to a considerable extent been dependant on the students' ideas and contributions.

Each of the above styles has their strengths and weaknesses. What is important to improved and effective teaching is to understand the differing styles and to begin to recognise when and where they are best deployed. Barnes suggests a framework that can be applied to student and lecturer participation in respect of teaching styles. Participation is seen as represented by three dimensions: that of closed, framed and negotiated behaviour.

Each dimension relates to content, focus, student role, key concepts and methods.

A *closed approach* is reflected in the following type of behaviour: tightly controlled by the lecturer; not negotiated; authoritative knowledge and skills; simplified monolithic. When using this approach the student's role becomes one of acceptance, routine performance with little or no access to principles. Key elements are considered to be those of authority: the proper procedures and the right answers. The most frequent method used to deploy such an approach is that of exposition: worksheets, note-giving, individual exercises and extended reading and routine practical work.

A *framed approach* would require the lecturer to control the subject/topic, frame reference and tasks, and make criteria explicit. The focus is one that stresses empirical testing: processes are chosen by the lecturer and some legitimisation is given to students' ideas. In this scenario the student's role is to join the lecturer's thinking and help in making hypotheses, set up tests, but always operate within the lecturer's framework. Key concepts are considered to be access to skills, processes and criteria; the method by which these are implemented rely on exposition, with discussion eliciting suggestions, individual/group problem solving, lists of tasks given and, discussion of outcomes, but the lecturer adjudicates.

A *negotiated approach* reflects a content that is discussed at each point and that students have a role in decision making. The main focus of this approach is to search for justifications and principles, giving students a strong legitimisation of their ideas. The student is allowed to discuss goals and methods critically, and share responsibility for frameworks and criteria. The key issues are that students see the relevance of what is being taught, have a voice in critical discussions and to set priorities to their learning. The method by which this is facilitated is by group and whole class discussion and decision making about goals and criteria. Students plan and carry out work, make presentations, and evaluate the success of the learning and teaching that has taken place.

Points for consideration

Use the above framework to decide the type of teaching style which most represents your approach to teaching and learning. Reflect on your decisions and identify possible changes you may wish to carry out.

Models of effective teaching

Effective teaching is concerned with how best to bring about desired learning outcomes and change the way students think by involving them in learning activities. Over the years research has devised a variety of models, contexts and scenarios that represent effective teaching. More recently there has been a consensus that there are some basic variables that affect teaching and learning environments. Figure 2.1 distinguishes between three variables which affect a teaching situation. A similar framework is discussed in terms of student learning in Chapter 3.

- *Context variables*: These relate to the characteristics of the context in which learning activities and teaching tasks take place. They include the lecturer's personality and the nature of the student body.
- *Process variables*: These relate to the characteristics of lecture and student behaviour and the teaching/learning tasks that take place and have bearing on the success of the learning outcomes.
- *Product variables*: These relate to the learning outcomes desired by the lecturer and the programme. They form the basis of either the lecturer's

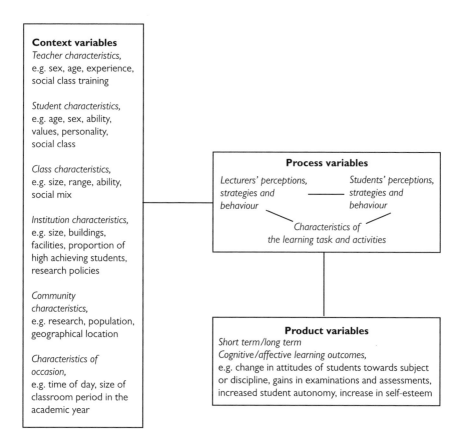

Figure 2.1 Framework for effective teaching

planning of the learning sessions and/or objectives or criteria which will be used to monitor effectiveness and student progress.

The above framework has been used in a number of ways to conduct research into effective teaching and learning. This chapter recognises the extent of this research but focuses on the pragmatic elements that can help the lecturer formulate strategies for effective teaching that best suit their discipline, personality and student body.

Three models of effective teaching

The various research in this area has asked the questions 'what' and 'how' effective teaching can be conceptualised. From these questions three models have been developed. These are closely connected to ways in which students learn. Chapter 3 explores the student's learning perspective in detail. Here the three models are considered in the context of developing teaching.

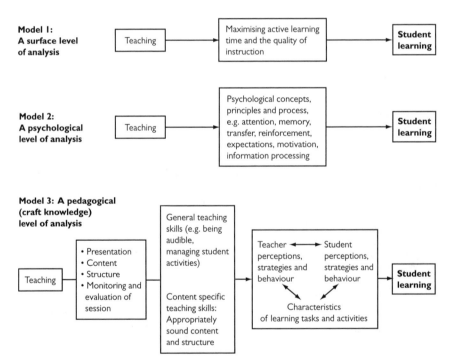

Figure 2.2 Models of effective teaching

Model 1: A surface level of analysis

The derivation of this model stems from work carried out by Anderson (1984) and Peterson and Walber (1979). This research has focused on two main constructs which are the key to effective teaching. The first construct is identified as *active learning time* (ATL); it refers to the amount of time spent by students actively engaged in a learning task or situation designed to achieve the stated learning outcomes. The second construct relates to *quality of instruction* (QI). This refers to the quality of the learning task or situation in terms of its appropriateness and suitability in achieving the stated learning outcomes. This model equates effective teaching with maximising ALT and QI. Within this, active learning focuses on the nature of each student's active mental engagement in the activities and environment provided by the lecturer. Adopting this approach allows the construct of quality instruction to complement active learning by emphasising it as bringing about the desired learning outcomes. The quality of the teaching and learning activities/environment themselves should be underpinned by the learning outcomes.

Quality of instruction in essence refers to the extent to which the instruction makes it easy for students to achieve the intended learning outcomes.

In order to achieve the learning outcomes in the way stated above, the lecturer has to consider if the learning experience being planned is organised in the most sound and appropriate ways when the characteristics of the students are taken into consideration (e.g. ability, prior knowledge, etc.). Quality instruction covers a variety of aspects and elements of instruction, the most significant of which is the lecturer's transactions with the students and the content, structure and organisation of the learning medium.

Model 2: A psychological level of analysis

This model stems from the consideration of psychological factors that may affect teaching and learning. The model extends the two constructs from Model 1, which in essences states that the processes of instruction have an influence on the learning outcomes. The psychological level of analysis links the process variables with the learning outcomes by explaining the influence psychological elements might have in the learning process and thus influence the nature of effective teaching.

The psychological level of analysis brings together the relationship between processes and psychological factors that are necessary to make learning happen. It focuses on the individual by considering the psychological processes involved in learning. There is a great deal of literature surrounding psychological theories of learning; however, a simple analysis would suggest that there are three main precepts that affect learning when thinking about effective teaching. These are:

1   The student must be *attending* to the learning experience.
2   The student must be *receptive to* the learning experience (i.e. being motivated or willing to learn and respond to the learning environment).
3   The learning experience must be *appropriate* for the desired learning outcomes (taking account of student's prior knowledge and understanding).

These three aspects are the basic conditions in which learning will take place. If effective teaching is to take account of psychological implications to learning the above three aspects have to be considered. The conditions of learning are a focus for developing teaching and learning.

Model 3: A pedagogical level of analysis

This model focuses on the craft of teaching and how this craft can be described in a way that it may be translated into experiences that enhance student learning. This model is based on teachers'/lecturers' understanding of what teaching is and how it may be interpreted to foster effective teaching and learning environments. It is practitioner based. This model sees teaching as managing activities and seeks to identify the major tasks of teaching associated with managing the learning environment. The main feature of the pedagogical model is that it focuses attention on aspects of teaching that are subjectively richer in meaning and significance than the types of process variables. This means that the model considers elements such as what constitutes teaching skills, and effective teaching. The main thrust has been to identify three basic categories that affect teaching and learning. These can be summarised as follows:

1   Teacher/lecturer perceptions, strategies and behaviour;
2   Student perception, strategies and behaviour;
3   Characteristics of learning tasks and activities.

The interrelationship of these elements will reflect the processes that occur within a teaching/learning environment. The implication is that a lecturer has to be aware both of their own perceptions and that of the student when setting and engaging in learning tasks and activities. These perceptions lead to certain types of behaviour and expectations. Understanding these issues will allow the lecturer to have a greater sense of what is happening and being achieved in their lecture room or classroom.

> **Points for consideration**
>
> Identify your prior conceptions of effective teaching and the implications these may have for the style of teaching you may wish to employ in your sessions. How do your perceptions of teaching influence your behaviour?

Constructing learning environments

A significant aspect when thinking about the development of teaching and learning situations is how to construct learning environments and establish how effective these are in terms of student achievement and the designated learning outcomes.

Chapters 3, 4, 5 and 6 give clear and explicit descriptions and examples of student learning, planning, etc.; what this chapter is aiming to do is to introduce the broad areas of development. Teaching style and models of teaching form the foundations of thinking in relation to learning environments, but it is equally important to know and understand how to construct a learning environment. These include issues such as:

- exposition;
- academic work;
- environment.

Exposition

The way students learn is directly related to the way they listen and think in response to lecturers' teaching styles, exposition, prompts and information. Exposition can be related to three main areas in terms of students' learning. These are:

1   Making clear the structure and purpose of the learning experience;
2   Informing, describing and explaining;
3   Using questions and discussion to facilitate and explore students' learning and understanding of concepts and knowledge.

Key to making things explicit is to emphasise the essential elements and areas of learning that students are required to engage in. This has often been explained as, 'tell the students what you are going to tell them, tell them and then tell them what you told them.' How this is transferred into a teaching situation is dealt with in chapters 4 and 5. The above statement can be taken to mean the how and why you brief and debrief students about their learning. This means making explicit what they are going to engage in, how they are to engage with the activity or information and what is expected of them once they have engaged with material. It is always easier to read a map if you know where you are starting from and where your destination is. Teaching is similar, and exposition is the key to reaching your destination.

Lecturer exposition has to include the giving, describing and explaining of knowledge, concepts and skills. At one extreme, lecturer exposition can constitute the only learning activity such as a lecture, and at the other, where the lecturer merely gives instruction on how the learning session is to be conducted. In both of these cases certain issues have to be taken into account. Psychologically students cannot pay attention for long periods of time; they will not absorb an hour's lecture in one go. Most students will take in information during the first ten minutes of a session. Hence exposition should take these factors into account. At the other extreme, students may well forget what was expected of them in terms of learning outcomes, hence requiring continual reinforcement and *aide-mémoires*. The essence of exposition is to strike a balance between information giving, asking questions, and encouraging discussion and problem solving, with reinforcement and motivation and attention gaining activities.

Questioning encourages students to:

- think, understand ideas, concepts, processes, phenomena and values;
- check their understanding, knowledge and skills;
- engage in dialogue with peers and lecturer;
- review and reflect on the level of their understanding;
- express their views and opinions as well as their understanding of what has been learned.

Academic work

This refers to the learning activities, tasks and experiences used by the lecturer in conjunction with lecturer exposition to engage students in their learning. The most important aspect here is understanding that students are constantly looking to make sense of what is expected of them by lecturers (cf. Chapter 3), as well as trying to gain success in the learning tasks set for them. Hence when planning academic work it is essential to think about how student success can be achieved. It is not good for the student to concentrate on how to perform successfully; it is more important for the student to concentrate on how to learn effectively. To help in the process of creating academic work for teaching, the following examples may be considered:

- structured reading and writing assignments;
- investigative and problem-based learning;
- individualised project-based learning;

- group work;
- experiential learning.

The above points are discussed in detail in Chapter 6.

Points for consideration

Consider your teaching style and identify the following aspects:

- What are the essential elements of your teaching exposition?
- Are they a valid way of approaching teaching?
- Does your exposition concentrate on student learning or on the giving of information?
- How often do you use questioning and discussion?

Concluding comments

This chapter has introduced the basic elements of developing teaching and learning. Each aspect identified is dealt with in greater depth throughout the book. The main aim has been to show the diversity of aspects that can affect teaching and learning within a given context. An appreciation of teaching style, models of teaching and learning environments is a key starting point for the development of effective teaching and learning. To date, much of the literature on effective teaching has relied on an image of higher education teaching that is traditional both in terms of teaching style and educational outcomes that are derived from performance assessment in the form of examinations. More recently there has been a significant push to change this image of teaching and learning in higher education. Greater diversity of teaching styles, techniques and activities, such as the inclusion of ICT, has had a significant bearing on how to change concepts of effective teaching. Hence thinking related to effective teaching needs to keep pace with a changing world of higher education, and what it means to teach and learn in higher education.

Chapter 3

Student learning

Introduction

The main aim of this chapter is to show the nature and importance of teaching effectiveness in the higher education setting. It will demonstrate how teaching and learning need to be considered together, and have an integral role to play in student achievement. The present role of the teacher in higher education and how this role is changing and acquiring a greater importance will be explored. At the heart of the discussion will be ideas related to the relationship between pedagogic practice and the various disciplines within higher education.

Teaching is a complex social activity; you create a course by manipulating a number of personal and cognitive variables that you hope will serve the welfare of your students. Becoming competent and proficient in the development of programmes and the subsequent teaching of them depends on a myriad of things, but particularly an understanding of how students learn. Stimulating students to think creatively and independently requires insight into learning styles. This chapter will concentrate on student learning from a variety of perspectives. In this way it hopes to introduce the lecturer to a range of theories that can create more effective learning environments for their students.

The teaching/learning framework

As a lecturer it is essential that you present information, ideas, concepts and knowledge in a way students can learn. This sounds a very commonsense statement, but it is of significant importance. The way students learn and the learning styles they adopt are all elements of the teaching and learning process that new lecturers need to be aware of. There is a vast literature on human learning from a variety of perspectives. Psychology and especially developmental psychology give insight into human behaviour and the thinking processes adopted by individuals. The processes can and do influence the learning outcomes of teaching/learning situations.

Students learn in different ways and it is important to understand the elements that constitute the basic learning processes. The environment significantly affects learning and the relationships created by the tutor and the student. It is therefore helpful to consider student learning within a theoretical framework. Three basic elements need to be considered. These include the social context, knowledge base, and psychological aspects.

1 *The social context*: describes the relationship between teaching and learning environments in the lecture room, lab, etc. and those that exist outside, such as ideology, and a particular way of thinking about learning at the time, such as information technology, culture and the higher education setting generally.
2 *Knowledge base*: This has a great bearing on the teaching strategies and learning activities and settings that might be used to facilitate student learning. Students come to the lecture room with different understandings and perceptions of the subject and knowledge bases to the lecturer.
3 *Psychological*: aspects particularly refer to theories of learning, and how lecturers learn from them and adapt them to best possible use in their teaching as a means of enhancing student learning.

Effective teaching and learning depends on the ability of the lecturer or tutor to create learning experiences that attain the learning outcomes of the programme or course being taught. Managing the learning process requires an understanding of students' learning and learning styles.

Every lecturer has a personal theory about how students learn and how they should be taught (Prosser and Trigwell, 1997). During teaching sessions the lecturer is frequently making judgements about the nature, quality and quantity of learning that is taking place and makes continuous judgements about the value of what is being learned. These judgements are frequently based on internal representations and personal constructs of how teaching should be conducted. If teaching is to improve and become effective, there is a need to understand the process of teaching and learning from a more theoretical perspective, thus enabling the lecturer to make more accurate judgements about the learning taking place within the session. To help this understanding it is important to stop and ask the questions: What do we mean by learning? How do students learn?

What do we mean by learning?

Understanding learning requires the consideration of a theoretical framework. This is greatly assisted by asking the following questions;

• How do students develop concepts and are there any theoretical structures that can assist the process?

- What mental processes do students engage in when they are trying to learn?
- What changes occur in the students' cognitive structures which themselves constitute student learning?
- What psychological factors (concepts, principles and processes) facilitate student learning?
- What are the main types of student learning?

Although theorists have elaborated their answers to the above questions in a variety of different ways, there are a number of convergent points within the separate approaches. It is therefore possible to establish a synthesis and consensus that can build into a framework for thinking about the nature of student learning.

Learning can be thought of as a change in student behaviour, which takes place as a result of being engaged in an educational experience. This is the fundamental premise on which Gagné (1985) based his conditions of learning that highlighted five main areas of student learning. These help when thinking about a teaching/learning framework. The five categories are:

1   *Intellectual skills.* These relate to 'knowing how' rather than 'knowing that'.
2   *Verbal skills.* These are associated with knowing names, places, and recalling principles and generalisations.
3   *Cognitive strategies.* These are ways in which students manage the mental processes (e.g. thinking and memorising).
4   *Attitudes.* These are concerned with students' emotions, and the social and cultural approaches to the subject and learning.
5   *Motor skills.* These are required for the physical tasks of learning, such as being able to use IT, chemical equipment or laboratory material.

These five aspects contribute to the task of learning and lead to a particular type of definition of learning as stated at the beginning of this section.

- *Verbal information* relates to facts, names, principles and generalisations.
- *Intellectual skills* relate to 'knowing how' rather than 'knowing that'. These can be arranged in increasing order of complexity as 'discriminations, concepts, rules and higher order rules', each of which is seen to build upon the less complex skill. Intellectual skills can be demonstrated by application to the different examples of the phenomena to which they refer.
- *Cognitive strategies* relate to ways in which students are able to control and manage the mental processes involved in learning. These include

strategies for attending, thinking and memorising and for dealing with novel problems.

- *Attitudes* can be defined as a student's feelings towards some particular object or class of objects. The fostering of attitudes such as those towards disciplines, workload, studying, learning, engagement and lecturers can be defined as an important educational outcome. Gagné emphasises the cognitive and behavioural aspects of attitudes as 'preference which influences personal action'.
- *Motor skills* relate to physical activities such as operating a computer, word processor, playing an instrument or manipulating equipment.

The elements put forward by Gagné are a starting point in considering the role of theory of learning and student learning outcomes. However, learning is complex, and psychological factors play a significant role in the development of learning, learning strategies and learning styles. Your students will demonstrate all of these factors in a very diverse way. Understanding the underlying principles of learning will be helpful in planning and developing teaching sessions for your students. If learning is to take place, tutors and lecturers have to give students the space and opportunities to make explicit their understanding and then to consider alternative approaches and hypotheses. This assumes that students become actively involved in their learning. If students are to become active learners, tutors have to facilitate this activity.

Consider the following statement:

> The most important single factor influencing learning is what the learner already knows; ascertain this and teach him/her accordingly.
> (Ausubel, 1968, p. 36)

This statement has been widely used in the field of education and training. Its interpretation has also been varied. Ausubel's treatment of types of learning emphasises two important distinctions in student learning. The first is a distinction between reception and discovery learning; the second is a distinction between rote and meaningful learning. Ausubel suggests that reception learning requires that the entire content of what is to be learned is presented to the learner in its final form; the student is required to internalise or incorporate the material present. This type of approach is often found in the standard lecture whereby the lecturer transmits all the information in one go, with students passively taking notes and not engaging with the material in any way. Discovery learning requires the student to be actively involved in learning by engaging and discovering what is to be learned through a specific learning activity. For the lecturer this might mean giving students problem-solving activities or tasks during a lecture or teaching session. The most significant form of learning is meaningful learning, where the essential characteristic of the learning is that it can be related in a meaningful, non-arbitrary way to what the learner already knows. Rote learning on the other hand is characterised by arbitrary associations with the student's previous knowledge.

Ausubel's interpretation of learning identifies some interesting points for the lecturer to consider. The two distinctions he makes – reception versus discovery learning and meaningful versus rote learning – are independent of each other. Hence reception learning can be meaningful or rote and discovery learning can also be meaningful or rote. This is an important distinction for planning teaching sessions, as there is often a belief that reception learning is also rote learning and that discovery learning is mean-ingful learning. The distinction that Ausubel makes allows the lecturer to plan a reception-orientated session that has meaningful learning as its aim. Meaningful learning has important implications for teaching for under-standing. Teaching for understanding emphasises the type of change required in cognitive structure by the student during the teaching/learning process. This approach gives pointers to the lecturer as to how one might think about student learning and apply strategies that might enhance student learning. Consider the following:

- Find the prior concepts understood by the learner and determine the necessary links between what is taught to what the learner already knows (Ausubel, 1968).
- Establish the meanings and concepts that the learner has already gener-ated from their background, attitudes, abilities and experiences and find ways to enable the learner to generate new meanings and concepts that will be useful to them (Wittrock, 1986).
- Find the subskills that a learner has and plan their learning to start from these subskills (Gagné and White, 1978).

The above interpretations all have merit and offer the lecturer a differing starting point to their teaching.

Points for consideration

Consider the topic you are about to teach, list the knowledge, concepts and skills you expect the students to know and those which you expect to develop within your session. Identify for yourself the connections between expectations of knowledge and the new knowledge you hope to develop for the students.

Lecturers expect their students to learn, and through the learning process to change their interpretations of the world in which they live through developing their understanding of the subject they are studying. However, this does not always happen. Students leave higher education with quantities of information/knowledge, yet change nothing about the way they understand what that information means. These are issues that must be addressed if teaching and learning are to become more effective and efficient. Bruner (1966) constructed a theory of instruction that put information processing by the learner at the heart of the theory. He suggested four basic elements that assist learning:

1   Learning involves a search for patterns, regularities and predictability.
2   Instruction serves to assist students in the formation and discovery of such patterns.
3   The above (2) is necessary if students' activities are transformed into symbolic rational thinking.
4   Action is the starting point for the formation of abstract symbolic thinking.

These four elements are represented in Figure 3.1.

The aspect of Bruner's theory that is useful when considering teaching and learning is that he concentrates on the different processes that are used in creative problem solving and emphasises that language, communication and instruction are paramount to the development of understanding and knowledge. The processes that are involved vary from individual to individual;

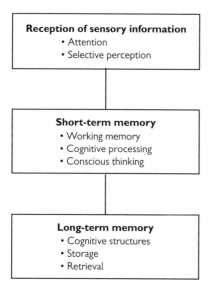

Figure 3.1 A basic interpretation of Bruner's information-processing model, which is associated with active learning

however, they underpin intelligent and adaptive thinking. For Bruner, learning involves the search for patterns, regularity and predictability. One aspect of the lecturer's role is to assist students in the formation and discovery of such patterns and rules, thus enhancing and expanding their knowledge. If this is the case how do students learn?

The central role of the student in the learning process

Bruner's theory gives us some indication of what learning involves and how the lecturer might assist that process, a process where the lecturer's role is to produce effective and independent learners. However, it is important to understand that both lecturer and student have a part to play in such a notion. Theories of learning imply that learning is essentially an interactive process. The action of the lecturer and the student determines the quality of the learning process that takes place. Hence one must consider the role of the student in the learning process and the activities and interactions associated with that learning.

The main use of theories of learning is to help lecturers improve their teaching and enhance student learning. The theories should act as a platform to help critical reflection and thus allow lecturers to construct their own understanding of the learning process. Students need to gain meaning and understanding from teaching; understanding cannot be imposed or transmitted by direct instruction. Understanding is gained through involvement in learning activities. Students' approaches to learning will have a direct bearing on their learning outcomes. Biggs (1999) explains this well. He suggests that 'what people construct from a learning encounter depends on their motives and intentions, on what they know already and how they use their prior knowledge. Meaning is therefore personal' (p. 13). He goes on to say that learning is thus a way of interacting with the world. As we learn, our conceptions of phenomena change, and we see the work differently. This approach to learning is often classified as constructivist. A constructivist perspective has clear implications for teaching and learning. Teaching becomes the vehicle for changing students' conceptions about phenomena and the world they engage in, and not about imparting or transmitting knowledge. Teaching becomes a way of facilitating students to think about new knowledge to restructure their conceptions. Lecturers should be aiming at conceptual change, not just the acquisition of information.

Conceptual change requires the altering of meaning to create a new cognitive structure. Cognitive reorganisation occurs as learners attempt to overcome obstacles or contradictions that arise as they engage in 'learning' activities. Conceptual change is a central tenet to the development of meaning. What is important for teaching is that students need to be given the opportunity to build up structures of new knowledge in a way that allows them to consider new knowledge relative to their pre-existing knowledge.

What then facilitates conceptual change? Conceptual change derives from a constructivist approach to learning, which defines learning as a process of personal construction of meaning. As such this offers a powerful way to rethink pedagogic practice. Incorporating a constructivist approach to pedagogic practice has implications for teaching and the activities associated with that teaching. Some of the implications for practice include the following:

- Lectures should provide instructional situations that bring forth students' subject/discipline activity.
- Students' actions should attempt to view students' solutions from the latter perspective.
- Lectures should recognise that what seem like errors and confusion indicate students' current thinking and understanding.
- Lecturers should realise that substantive learning occurs in periods of conflict, confusion, surprise, over long periods of time and during social interactions.

From this perspective, teaching is viewed as far more than providing information and checking/testing to see if it has been acquired by the students. Instead, teaching becomes a matter of creating situations in which students actively participate in activities that enable them to make their own individual constructions. Activities such as open discussion, group work and problem solving greatly enhance conceptual change and individual construction. Allowing students to discuss and interact openly gives the lecturer opportunities to guide the students to higher levels of construction and abstraction. The main aim of such activities is to encourage students to explain their ideas and to try and understand the thinking of others. The lecturer's role is to help the students to examine the differences between the views and ideas the students have offered.

Teaching in this way perceives learning as allowing the student to participate in normative activities which are shared (Rogoff, 1990). From this perspective meanings are mutually constructed during social interaction, and which evolve from the students' interpretations as well as contributions from the lecturer.

How do students learn?

What motivates student learning? In order to answer this question it is important to bear in mind a clear distinction between learning that takes place by the individual as a natural aspect of interacting with the environment and peers and the specific learning which is intended by the lecturer during a teaching session. When asking the question, What motivates student learning?, one is really asking about the ways in which students make a positive mental contribution towards the learning tasks and teaching session in which they have to engage. What is important is that students are both intrinsically motivated and extrinsically motivated to learn. Figures 3.2–3.4 show the various models of student learning and approaches to learning that can influence student achievement. These motivations refer respectively to the expectations students have of them. The two categories respond to learning because they are interested in the work and learning and because they

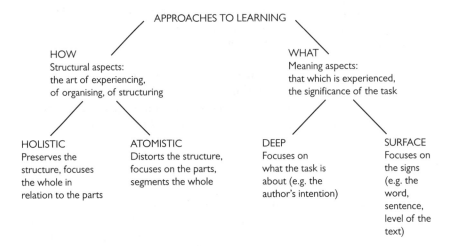

Figure 3.2 Approaches to learning

Source: Based on Figure 1 in Marton (1988), p. 66 (taken from Ramsden, 1992).

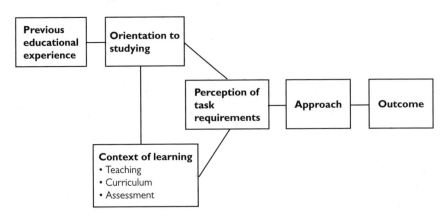

Figure 3.3 Student learning in context

Source: Ramsden (1992).

Study orientation	Approach	Style	Stereotypic personality	Processes	Probable outcomes
Meaning orientation	Deep active	Versatile	Integrated and balanced personality	Uses evidence critically, argues logically and interprets imaginatively	Describing, justifying and criticising what was learned. High grades with understanding
Meaning orientation	Deep passive	Comprehension learning	Impulsive introvert with a theoretical orientation	Intuitive imaginative, thriving on personal interpretation and integrative overview but neglecting evidence	Mentioning overall argument, laced with illustration and anecdote. (Fairly high grades in arts)
Reproducing orientation	Surface active	Operation learning	Converger with strong economic and vocational interests	Attention to detail, cautious and limited interpretation, syllabus bound and anxiously aware of assessment demands	Accurately describing fact and components of arguments, but not related to any clear overview
Non-academic orientation	Surface passive	Improvidence combined with globe-trotting	Social extrovert with few academic interests or vocational aspirations	Little attention to detail, over readiness to generalise, superficial treatment and casual interpretation	Mentioning often irrelevant facts within a disordered haphazard overview. (Low grades)
Strategic orientation	Deep or surface approach as necessary	Strategic	Stability and confidence combined with competitive aggressiveness	Detail or meaning as perceived to be required by lecturer	High grades, with or without understanding

Figure 3.4 Framework of descriptions of student learning Entwistle and Ramsden
Source: Ramsden (1992).

have to. Intrinsic motivation stems from an inward drive of curiosity. It involves an interest in the learning task itself and the satisfaction of being involved in and learning from that task. Extrinsic motivation refers to learning situations where the impetus for the motivation stems from satisfying a personal drive, where the learning task is seen to be a means to an end, such as formalised assessment. Intrinsic and extrinsic motivations have clear implications for teaching sessions. Ramsden (1992) takes this further in relation to deep and surface learning.

Learning theories can provide ideas about the types of activities or interactions which encourage students to have a positive mental approach to their learning. There is a distinction between the nature and the context of the learning intended by the teacher and the learning actually experienced by the student. Students have to be both interested and actively involved in what they do to maximise learning. The way one goes about learning is a relationship between the person and the material being learned (Ramsden, 1992). For students to be able to engage in their learning in such a way, the lecturer needs to be aware of the following points:

- how the individual makes sense of a learning situation or assignment;
- understand that this involves the learning of 'something';
- understand that there is no such thing as 'learning' in itself;
- understand that the concept of approaches to learning describes a qualitative aspect of learning;
- understand how students' experiences influence their learning and organise the subject matter of a learning task, i.e. the how and the what they are to learn.

The most influential research over the past twenty years about how students learn has been the concept of 'approaches to learning'. This concept requires an understanding that the way individuals go about learning is a relationship between the individual and the material being learned. It requires an appreciation that the relationship between the individual and the material being learned depends on how the individual makes sense of a particular learning assignment, task or activity. In this context learning is always related to learning something. The concept of approach describes a qualitative aspect of learning. It is about how individuals experience and organise the subject matter or learning task; it is about 'what' and 'how' they learn, rather than how much they remember (Ramsden, 1992). An underlying implication from approaches to learning is that whatever any one student learns, he or she will relate to different tasks in different ways.

Deep approach to learning

Deep approach to learning is exemplified as an intention to understand and seek meaning, leading students to attempt to relate concepts to existing experiences distinguishing between new ideas and existing knowledge and critically evaluating and determining key themes and concepts. Students aim to achieve maximum meaning from their studying, which is achieved by high levels of cognitive processing throughout the learning activity. Facts are learned in the context of meaning.

This approach can be summarised in the following way:

- Intention to understand.
- Student maintains structure of task.
- Focus on 'what is signified' (e.g. the author's argument or the concepts applicable to solving the problem).
- Relate previous knowledge to new knowledge.
- Relate theoretical ideas to everyday experience.
- Relate and distinguish evidence and argument.
- Organise and structure content into a coherent whole. *Internal* emphasis. 'A window through which aspects of reality become visible and more intelligible.'

(Entwistle and Marton, 1984)

What do these elements mean to the lecturer and how can they be adapted to improve teaching sessions? Lecturers may wish to consider how deep approaches to learning may be encouraged.

Deep approaches are encouraged by:

- Teaching and assessment methods that foster active and long-term engagement with learning tasks.
- Stimulating and considerate teaching, especially teaching which demonstrates the lecture's personal commitment to the subject matter and stresses its meaning and relevance to students.
- Clearly stated academic expectations.
- Opportunities to exercise responsible choice in the method and content of study.
- Interest in and background knowledge of the subject matter.
- Previous experiences of educational settings that encourage these approaches.

Surface approach to learning

This approach is exemplified as an intention to complete the task, memorise information and facts, make no distinction between new ideas and existing knowledge, and to treat the task as externally imposed. Rote learning is a typical strategy adopted by surface learners. Students also give the impression that they are seriously involved with the learning that is taking place, which is achieved through superficial levels of cognitive processing. In this approach students are concerned only with completing task requirements. Students also tend to distort the structure of the task. Students:

- Focus on the signs (e.g. the words and sentences of the text, or unthinkingly on the formula needed to solve the problem).
- Focus on unrelated parts of the task.
- Memorise information for assessments.
- Associate facts and concepts unreflectively.
- Fail to distinguish between principles and examples.
- Treat task as an external imposition.

External emphasis: such as demands of assessments, knowledge cut off from everyday reality, lead to surface approaches to learning that are encouraged by the following activities and settings:

- Assessment methods emphasising recall or the application of trivial procedural knowledge.
- Assessment methods that create anxiety.
- Cynical or conflicting messages about rewards.
- An excessive amount of material in the curriculum.
- Poor or absent feedback on progress.
- Lack of independence in studying.
- Lack of interest in and background knowledge of subject matter.
- Previous experiences of educational settings that encourage these approaches.

Learning styles

Students tend to adopt particular strategies for learning; these are referred to as 'learning styles'. The holistic style is called 'comprehension learning', which involves building descriptions of what is known. The serialist style is called 'operation learning', which is the facet of the learning process concerned with mastering procedural details. Students with different learning styles appear to be drawn to different subject areas (Entwistle, 1982). These descriptions by Entwistle were further developed by Wolf and Kolb (1984), who suggest that students develop different learning styles which emphasise preference for a certain mode of learning. Wolf and Kolb suggests four categories of learning style.

1 Convergent learning. The strengths of this style lie in practical application of ideas, where the dominant learning ability is considered to be
active experimentation and abstract conceptualisation.
2 Divergent learning has strengths in the generation of ideas and allowing
the imaginative ability to be developed. The dominant learning ability is
considered to be concrete experience and reflective observation.
3 Assimilative learning focuses on the creation of theoretical models
and making sense of disparate observations. The dominant learning
ability is considered to be abstract conceptualisation and reflective
observation.
4 Accommodative learning allows students to carry out plans and tasks
that involve them in new experiences. The dominant learning style is
considered to be a concrete experience and active participation.

It is important to understand the differences between deep and surface
approaches to academic tasks in terms of students' intentions. The deep
approach is internal to the content of the problem and to the knowledge,
experience and interests of the learner. The surface approach is external to
the task and its requirements, and implies a process of learning in which
alien material is to be impressed on the memory for a limited period of time,
and with the specific intention of satisfying external demands.

Applying learning styles and approaches to teaching

When thinking about improving student learning it is important to understand and consider how individuals learn and approach their studying. The
above discussion has shown that it is possible to identify common constituent
elements, which include the acceptance that the learning process varies at
individual levels, and that the student will develop a learning style and refine
that style in response to three generalised factors. The three factors constitute the following elements:

- unconscious personal interventions by the individual;
- conscious interventions by the learner;
- interventions by some external agent.

The term 'learning style' has evolved as a practical means of explaining
student interactions during teaching and learning sessions. Such practical explanations have application to education and training programmes. Riding
and Cheema (1991) suggest that the term 'learning styles' has replaced
the term 'cognitive style', and that cognitive style is only one part of an
individual's learning style. Thus learning style can be taken to mean an
understanding of the whole processes undertaken during a learning activity.
Keefe and Ferrell (1990, p. 16) suggest that a learning style is:

> A complexus of related characteristics in which the whole is greater than its parts. Learning style is a gestalt combining internal and external operations derived from the individual's neurobiology, personality and development, and reflected in learner behaviour.

If the above statement is accepted, a learning style can be taken to mean the general tendency towards a particular learning approach displayed by an individual student. How then can this information be used pragmatically to help in understanding the teaching and learning process?

The first is to understand that much of the research quoted above has shown the bipolar nature of student learning approaches. Kolb (1976) suggested that an individual might display a preference for one of four possible learning styles (cf. Chapter 8), but that these four styles derive from two dimensions presented as opposing elements of learning.

Robotham (1999) suggested that learning styles had a bipolar construction. This construction involved comparing theories of learning with high- and low-quality learning styles. His analysis suggests that the following theories offer a bipolar construction. Witkin (1977) puts forward the idea that high learning is field-independent and that low learning is field-dependent. Ausubel *et al.* (1968) regard the bipolar construction as meaningful learning and rote learning, whereas Goldman and Warren (1972) put forward the idea of logical learning and mnemonic learning. Wittrock (1986) makes the case for generative and reproductive learning. Following Wittrock's view, Pask (1976) classified learning as comprehensive and operational. The bipolar theory that has had most impact on teaching and learning has been that of Marton and Saljo (1976); their classification of deep and surface learning is constantly referred to in teaching and learning contexts. Robotham's analysis clearly shows that the variety of learning theories put forward have many common elements that can be placed under the broad heading of *quality learning*. He states: 'A key feature of these quality learning styles is that the learner approaches learning from a contextual perspective, where a problem is addressed at two levels, micro and macro.' At the micro level the problem or task requirements are addressed and completed, while at the macro level the problem or task is perceived in the context of the course or subject area of which it is a part (p. 2).

The useful transference to teaching here is that a basic division between types of learning outcomes can be appreciated; for example:

- *Low-quality learning* is associated with concentrating only on solving a particular problem or issue, not seeing the whole or engaging with the fact that the given problem is linked in any way with any prior learning or context given within the subject area that the problem has been set.

- *High-quality learning* is associated with the learner identifying links with other problems or issues in the same area. The individual actively makes these links by engaging with the learning process.

Effective teaching as described in chapter 2 requires an understanding of learning styles. Earlier in this chapter there has been discussion in relation to students' engagement with learning resting on the nature and context of the learning tasks set by the lecturer. The key question is, 'Does the fact that learning style can be divided into two broad areas mean that teaching tasks have to be divided in the same way?' This in essence would be a very narrow approach to learning tasks. Research is currently being undertaken to see how learning tasks affect learning outcomes (Nicholls, 2001). It is important to appreciate that each learning task or learning situation devised by a lecturer will have its own particular requirements and identity. It would be inappropriate to think that there are only two types of learning tasks. Serious thought must go into whether you wish to adopt a teaching style that matches a learning style. Not all students in your group may adopt the style you wish to put forward. Hence each teaching/learning session needs to be planned in such a way that maximises all potential learning styles.

Research in the area of match and mismatch of learning styles to teaching tasks is divided into two distinct sections. It is worth considering the literature here. Table 3.1 shows the research into matching learning styles and teaching styles, and Table 3.2 shows the literature related to how students adapt their behaviour to respond to the learning situation. The literature put forward is to show the extent to which the subject has been researched. It is also there for those who wish to learn more about student learning and learning styles. The research listed in tables 3.1 and 3.2 suggests that

Table 3.1 Research into matching learning styles and teaching styles

Learning is more effective where there is a match	Learning is more effective where there is a mismatch
Di Stefano (1970)	Gehlman (1951)
Koran et al. (1971)	Glass (1967)
Grieve and Davis (1971)	Coop and Brown (1971)
James (1973)	Anderson (1972)
Carpenter et al. (1976)	Nelson (1972)
McCleod and Adams (1977)	Montgomery (1972)
Witkin (1977)	Thornell (1974)
Hudak (1985)	Gorton (1975)
Canino and Cockerill (1988)	Kolb (1985)
Matthews (1991)	
Dunn et al. (1990)	
Hayes and Allinson (1996)	

Table 3.2 Literature related to how students adapt their behaviour to respond to the learning situation

Students adapt behaviour	Change learning through course of study
Messick (1984)	Barris *et al.* (1985)
Streufert and Nogami (1989)	
Talbot (1985)	
Standing and Sheevels (1994)	

students adapt to the teaching situation by changing or adapting their learning styles to match the particular learning situation they find themselves in.

What is important to the debate is whether or not a lecturer chooses to change his or her teaching style to match those of the students. A summary of the cited research would suggest that learning style is not a stable construct. A student's learning style might alter with teaching style as a mechanism for meeting his or her learning needs. This change in learning style will then require the lecturer to change their teaching style to meet the needs of the students; thus the cycle of learning style and teaching style continues. It is important for the effective teacher to recognise such cycles of teaching and learning and consequently to plan teaching sessions according to student group and subject area. What is clear is that there are a variety of factors which affect the learning process; choice of teaching strategy is merely one aspect. A major point for consideration is adaptability and flexibility on behalf of the lecturer who wishes to teach his or her students effectively.

Such flexibility requires lecturers to move away from traditional stimulus–response conditioning approaches, in which the learner is passive and trained to perform in a set manner in defined situations. The lecturer should aim for a stimulus–stimulus approach, where students and lecturer are actively involved in both learning and the mechanisms of the learning process. The lecturer should aim to facilitate learner autonomy and empowerment by developing the students' critical awareness of the material being studied and the delivery and structure of that material. If such flexibility and adaptability is gained by the lecturer, learners can then attempt to tailor their learning strategies to the requirements to optimise the quality of their own learning and the learning experience they find themselves in. The student should be encouraged to develop effective learning strategies. A proficient learner is not someone who demonstrates capability within a narrow band of activities, as defined by a particular learning style, but rather someone who demonstrates the ability to select an appropriate learning style from a range, according to the demands of the situation and their own learning (Robotham, 1999, p. 6). The value to the lecturer of learning styles is an appreciation that direct matching of teaching style to learning style is prag-matically inappropriate. However, an expectance that a variety of learning styles will exist with any given body of students is essential. To plan for a diverse set of students in terms of learning style, ability and prior knowledge is more effective. Merely deciding to do the standard lecture because it is the easiest way forward is not effective teaching. The students should not see the lecturer as being inflexible and a significant barrier to their learning, as the lecturer is often seen by the student as being the expert in their field and a key element to helping them develop their subject knowledge, and hence their learning, in the field.

The above descriptions and explanations can help the lecturer to under-stand the types of learning students engage with. The distinction between high-quality and low-quality learning orientation of students' learning styles can highlight for the lecturer the nature and context of activities that can be given to students. Students relying on reproducing information allow staff to define learning tasks and are interested in courses mainly for the qualifica-tion they offer. In contrast, students looking for meaning are interested in the work itself and interact critically with what they are learning. The implica-tions for improving teaching are significant. Teaching and learning must be seen as a collaborative venture. Good teaching does not necessitate effective learning but it should go a long way towards assisting the learning process.

To teach well requires:

- good planning and preparation;
- clear aims and objectives to teaching sessions;
- clear understanding of where individual sessions fit into a curriculum or series of teaching sessions;
- clear understanding of student levels, abilities and prior knowledge;
- well-prepared and organised resources;
- an enthusiasm and belief in what you are doing.

Good teaching encourages:

- high-quality student learning;
- active engagement with subject content;
- engaging with students at their level of learning;
- explaining material plainly;
- making clear what has to be understood, at what level and why;
- respect for students and encouraging student independence;
- giving high-quality feedback on student work;
- learning from students about the effects of your teaching and how it can be improved.

Approaches to learning and learning outcomes: What are the implications for teaching?

Deep and surface learning are responses to educational environments in which students find themselves. Ramsden states quite clearly that 'what students learn is indeed closely associated with how they go about learning it' (1992, p. 53). Research seems to indicate that students who take a deep approach to learning are closely correlated to better grades and higher quality learning outcomes. A deep approach is found to be related to perceptions that there is a choice in what is to be learned, that teaching is of high quality, and that there are clear goals and standards for what is to be learned.

What is important to appreciate here is that students adapt to the requirements they perceive lecturers expect of them. They usually try to please their lecturers, and do what they think will bring them rewards within the system. Prosser and Trigwell (1997) categorised this and other typical behaviour into three areas: presage, process and product (the 3P model). In this model students' perceptions of the learning and teaching context are seen to be an interaction between their previous experiences of learning and teaching and the learning and teaching context itself. Presage factors are twofold: the first relates to student factors and the second to teaching factors.

- *Student factors include*: prior knowledge, students' interest in the topic, and their commitment to university and learning.
- *Teaching factors include*: what is intended to be taught, how it will be taught and assessed, teachers' knowledge base and expertise, and the teaching/learning environment.

These factors all interact at the process level and influence the nature of the learning engaged in as to whether it is surface or deep learning. A consequence of this interaction is the nature of the learning outcome which can be thought of as quantitative, i.e. facts and skills, and qualitative, such as structure, transfer and active involvement. Biggs (1999) suggests that the 3P model describes teaching as a balanced system in which all components support each other (p. 25). For the model to function correctly all aspects of the model must align. Non-alignment suggests inconsistencies and unmet expectations. The context that is set for teaching depends on the following elements:

- the curriculum that is taught;
- the teaching methods selected;
- the assessment procedures selected;
- the feedback procedure implemented;

- the climate created between teacher and student;
- institutional expectations, rules and regulations.

Conclusion

Learning styles and approaches to learning are only part of the aspects related to student learning. The content and context in which students have to learn must also be taken into account. Students often adopt flexible strategies to cope with different academic demands. Marton suggests that the approaches to learning adopted by students should not characterise that student, but be seen as a response to a learning situation they find themselves in. The natural approach is a deep one (Marton, 1976). The most significant factor in student learning is an appreciation by the tutor/lecturer that a student's perception of what is required by the lecturer will determine the type of learning style and approach the student will engage in. The student's interest in the subject matter of the task is a crucial element of the deep approach to learning, as is the individual lecturer. The attitudes and enthusiasm of a lecturer, his or her concern for helping the students understand, and particularly his or her ability to understand the difficulties experienced by students in dealing with a new topic, will all affect the learning approaches adopted by the student. The most significant element affecting student learning is assessment. Research has shown that the way students are assessed in higher education tends to push them towards surface learning (cf. Chapter 4).

The difficulty for the lecturer is to obtain a balance, allowing for sufficient flexibility for the support of individual learning but also maintaining a structure where a whole group of students can be kept on track and allowed to learn and develop through a course, module or entire programme. Student autonomy and self-directed learning supported by the lecturer would seem to be an encouraging step forward. What the lecturer should be looking for is to move beyond the enhancement of student performance within a narrow spectrum of learning activities and teaching situations and the development of foundation skills, such as self-directed learning and learning autonomy.

Chapter 4

Planning and preparation

Introduction

This chapter demonstrates and discusses issues related to planning and preparation focusing on the development of sessions/lectures, and how evidence of such development may be documented. It will show how personal philosophies of teaching and learning can affect teaching strategies, and how the role of aims and objectives/learning outcomes relate to planning and teaching. The chapter will demonstrate that although there are generic approaches to teaching and learning, each discipline has its own identity, values and ethos, and as such impinges on perceptions and delivery of that discipline. Of equal importance in this chapter is the discussion related to the challenges faced by lecturers when delivering to very large numbers. Planning and preparation become paramount in such situations, as do the knock-on effects, such as student access to tutors and marking timetables, all of which require planning and preparation.

Planning and managing teaching sessions

Good practice reflects well-planned and managed teaching sessions, demonstrating effective student learning and engagement. Planning teaching and session management cannot be divorced from the aims and learning outcomes, module specifications and subject knowledge. One of the keys to effective teaching is good planning. A well-constructed and planned session is much more likely to produce effective student learning than an ill-prepared session.

Planning: key elements

There are four stages involved in planning and delivering a successful session, as shown in Figure 4.1.

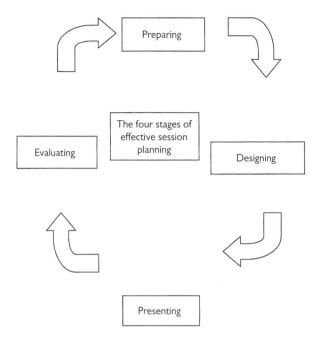

Figure 4.1 The four stages of effective session planning

1 Preparing

Preparation will involve understanding the intended learning outcomes of the course or module for the students in relation to the subject knowledge required for the particular session as well as determining the session aims, objectives and outcomes. It will involve research on the activities that may be appropriate for the session and the links required to the overall programme specifications.

2 Designing

The design of the session is crucial to its success. There should be variety, and the session must motivate the students and maintain their interest.

3 Presenting

Presenting the session requires thinking about:

• The timing of each section within the session.
• The way in which the structure of your session is implemented.

- The variety and extent to which the activities you have chosen for your session need direction from you.
- How your instructions are to be related to your students.
- Where appropriate, the need to consider health and safety aspects.

4 Evaluating

Evaluation is a means to understanding the effects of teaching on students' learning. It requires the collection of information about the teaching one is involved with, interpreting the information and making judgements about which actions should be taken to improve practice. Tutors, for the benefit of their professional competence and their student's understanding, should conduct evaluation. Evaluation requires the tutor to:

- Reflect on what helps students to understand a concept or argument, and to apply the results to teaching.
- Experiment with new ways of assessing students, and to monitor its effects on the quality of their learning.
- Listen to students describing their approach to learning a topic.
- Be involved in an analytical process that is intrinsic to good teaching.

Evaluating the success of a session or the reasons for failure of a session provides many pointers when designing future learning environments. The idea of the tutor as a reflective practitioner and a professional capable of learning from their experiences, both positive and negative, should not be underestimated.

The planning process

Before deciding the nature, context and learning activities that students will attempt in a session, the tutor must have a clear perspective as to the aim and purpose of the session that is going to be planned. Clear objectives and learning outcomes are needed. It may well be that the session being planned is one of a series of sessions that form the scheme of work for the module or topic under consideration. In a foundation programme the topic may form part of a multidisciplinary approach to a theme. In a postgraduate programme it is more likely to form part of a specialised and specific topic area. As well as the purpose of the session, the planning must take into account the context in which that session will be taught (e.g. as a practical session in science, art or music), as part of a syllabus in order to assess students against predetermined criteria, or as a theoretical session delivering subject knowledge. Session planning takes place within the agreed programme, course or module.

Planning learning environments and sessions must have short-, medium-

and long-term learning outcomes/objectives linked to them. Short-term planning (e.g. sessions, parts of sessions or short sequences of sessions) will be much of the day-to-day work of the academic tutor. This must take place within a framework of medium- and long-term planning. The medium-term may be a topic or unit of work that will last for part or even the whole of a module. This, in turn, will be subsumed in the long-term plan that may be based on part of a programme or complete degree programme.

The planning process must take into account the type of information gleaned from the students and the tutor's own reflections and evaluations of the sessions. It is essential to recognise the need for using assessment and evaluation evidence in future planning.

The care taken in planning sessions is more often than not reflected in their success in practice. A poorly planned session is rarely successful. It may occur without incident and the students may not necessarily fall asleep or walk out; however, the learning experience for the student will almost certainly be limited and narrowly focused. When preparing a session, try to be clear about the nature and context of the learning you anticipate will occur through your session or series of sessions. Learning was discussed in detail in Chapter 2. Here, five categories of learning are given to help identify the types of learning students might engage in and how best these may be utilised in the planning of the tasks to take place in your session. The five types are taken from Saljo (1982).

1   A qualitative increase in knowledge.
2   Memorising.
3   Acquisition of facts, methods, etc. which can be retained and used when necessary.
4   The abstraction of meaning.
5   An interpretation process aimed at understanding reality.

The above five categories fall into two further categories that are very useful in helping planning and preparation of sessions. These relate to cognitive learning which include categories 1, 2 and 3. These can be measured in terms of recall and retention. The second grouping includes categories 4 and 5. These offer a more holistic description of learning and coincide with the learning outcomes you would expect from your sessions.

In the planning stage it is important to construct a framework for what and how you are going to teach in your session. The process is the same whether it is in a lab or a lecture. Each of the five categories needs consideration in terms of whether you expect your students to recall facts or procedures at the end of the session or whether you expect them to go away with skills such as interpretation and analysis. Below is a framework that can help plan a teaching session or series of sessions.

Planning framework

Some of the suggested headings and areas for development within a given teaching plan are listed below.

- teaching session;
- date of session;
- module session taken from;
- aims of session;
- learning outcomes.

Session framework

1 Introduction

Every session should have a brief introduction that:

- Recaps previous work.
- Identifies students' knowledge and preconceptions.
- Directs the students to the content, purpose and learning outcomes of the session.

2 Knowledge base

Every session will have a knowledge base:

- Establish how much content you need to get through in the given time.
- Identify how much of the content is factual and recall, and how much needs explaining
- Can any of the factual material be given as a handout, thus leaving more time for knowledge application and explanation?

3 Session activities

To keep students motivated, each session should be divided into sections with activities to re-interest students and regain their attention. This is particularly the case with long lectures.

- Construct activities to match the session flow; for example, introduction, knowledge base, application and explanation of knowledge, understanding, concluding activity.
- These activities can be small and short; for example, instead of talking through an activity, set a problem and invite a student to explain the solution. In a lecture you can get students to discuss a problem briefly by

asking alternate rows to turn and talk to each other, then ask for views at the end of the task time.

4 Concluding the session

Every session should have a definitive concluding section. The tutor should round up all facts and learning objectives that should have been gained from the session. Students should also be directed as to the expected workload from the session. This could be pre-prepared on a sheet and handed out. The key to a conclusion of a session is that students are clear about the following:

- What they should have learned.
- What is expected from them following the session.
- What paperwork/reading is expected from them.
- The focus of the teaching session.
- The knowledge, facts, etc. they should take away with them.

The above suggested framework is a guideline to planning. Preparation is the essence of good, effective and efficient teaching. Use the framework to help plan single sessions or a series of sessions.

Teaching and managing the learning environment

This is a crucial aspect of effective teaching. Claxton (1984) defines teaching as 'what one person does to try and help another to learn' (p. 211). This broad definition includes a number of the activities that people most often associate with the act of teaching:

- Demonstrating skills.
- Giving friendly advice.
- Explaining things.
- Transferring information.
- Developing a knowledge base.

Bearing these five areas in mind, a prime consideration for tutors is how learners actually learn. 'If tutors do not understand what learning is, and how it happens, they are as likely to hinder as to help' (p. 212). Effective teaching may be thought of as the students successfully achieving the learning outcomes intended by the tutor. However, the key player in this is the tutor. The tutor has to understand that for learning to occur, the environment in which learning is meant to take place, whether this be a lecture theatre, classroom or laboratory, is the responsibility of the tutor, and as such must have a sense of coherent structure and order. The emphasis here is that sound session management is the key to success. The creation of a positive learning atmosphere requires students to be motivated, active and to feel valued within their learning space. To facilitate such an environment the tutor's role is to set high expectations of students. Many problems experienced by tutors are related to boredom, inactivity or a pace of a session being either too slow or too fast. Students often complain of boredom during sessions or where sessions had been conducted at such a pace that they had no notion of what they were learning. Boredom or lack of student engagement is often precipitated by badly planned and executed teaching sessions.

Good tutors are aware of this and will vary their teaching methods to keep students engaged in their learning and work. Developing an arsenal of teaching strategies, methods and styles is essential to becoming an effective academic teacher.

Exploring the meaning and underlying processes associated with teaching, planning and managing a learning session

What does 'teaching and session management' mean? Here the classroom is taken to be any space in which teaching and learning is to take place. Effective classroom management can be interpreted and viewed as one of the main elements in effective learning. Session management encompasses all the arrangements a tutor has to make in order to establish and maintain an environment in which students can learn, for example, effective organisation and presentation of sessions so that students are actively engaged in learning.

Establishing an effective learning environment

Establishing an effective learning environment requires the tutor to understand that there is a difference between managing students and managing learning. Each requires a different set of skills. Therefore, the establishment and sustainability of an effective learning environment is due to a number of predominantly proactive rather than reactive decisions made by the tutor. The tutor needs to understand how and what students require in order for them to learn within a pre-specified environment. These include:

- An understanding of what each group/set or individual needs to achieve the learning outcomes.
- The ability to facilitate each student's reflection upon learning.
- Allowing students to become autonomous learners.
- Allowing students to question each other and the tutor.
- Allowing feedback on group learning activities.

- Facilitating active rather than passive learning.
- Encouraging extended learning outside of the session.

These points can be facilitated within a set of rules and routines developed by the tutor and agreed with the students.

Rules and routines within session management

Brophy's (1983) term 'proactive problem prevention' is one which highlights the need for advanced planning and detailed consideration by the tutor regarding the kind of learning environment that they wish to establish and maintain not only in each individual session, but over a period of time.

What are the rules and routines in the context of session or class management? Rules identify general expectations of behaviour that cover a variety of situations (Siedentop, 1991, p. 95). A rule defines general expectations of acceptable and unacceptable behaviour that will cover different situations; for example, expecting students to be quiet and attentive when the tutor is talking, to respect other students' views and perceptions, meeting assignment deadlines, etc. Rules must remain flexible, so that they can react effectively to the changing circumstances of the context; that is, the interrelationship between the tutor, student and the learning environment. However, the tutor must endeavour to enforce rules on a continual basis. Tutors also need to consider the extent to which they intend to specify consequences for rule violations, and this element becomes increasingly important with QAA requirements of tracking student progress. Once again, these decisions will have a bearing on the way in which the relationship between the tutor and the students will be framed and maintained, and consequently the nature of their planning.

Points for consideration

- How are late submissions dealt with within the programme or course that you are teaching?
- Are there clear guidelines for resubmission?
- Are all students treated the same, or do they realise that there is a lack of consistency within the framework of extensions and resubmission?

One way whereby session management may be facilitated is by setting up learning routines for the students. Routines can be thought of as a compromise between the students' and tutor's expectations, within the framework of institutional rules and regulations. Siedentop (1991, p. 95) identifies routines as procedures for performing specific behaviours within a class, particularly those behaviours that regularly recur. For example, what are the rules and expectations regarding student attendance and punctuality; how could or should a tutor deal with the student who is continually late or does not attend sessions on a regular basis? If expectations and routines are established from the very beginning of a course, module or series of teaching sessions, and subsequently systematically maintained, a good working and learning environment will be established. The effective use of routines can save a great deal of learning time and minimise disruption within the context of the session. However, if they are to be effective they need to have the consent of the students. This consent is facilitated by a clear rationale shared between the tutor and the students. A learning environment that is governed by accurately, planned, open and well-understood routines is more likely to be a productive one.

Points for consideration

When thinking of a teaching session or series of sessions with students, what strategies may be useful in order to:

- manage work and movement (getting students on task);
- manage relationships and reinforcing expectations of attitudes and behaviour;
- gaining attention – for students and the tutor (verbal and non-verbal cues);
- creating a trusting and motivating learning environment?

To assist the tutor in producing an effective and well-managed learning environment for students, the following points should be considered:

- Prepare the session: clearly identify learning outcomes in advance.
- Mark assignments: meeting deadlines and positive, useful feedback associated with motivation of students.
- Check the working space: is it available, suitable and safe to use?
- Check all equipment: is it readily available and in good order?
- Establish routines for attendance and code of behaviour in sessions.
- Have resources ready to use in the appropriate place (e.g. visual aids, hand out additional materials, etc.).

A positive climate for learning

The climate set-up in the lecture theatre, lab or studio, facilitated by the tutor, will have a significant effect on the nature of the learning environment. Embroiled in the creation and maintenance of a positive learning environment are a number of interrelating factors. A distinction can be drawn between teaching *qualities* and *tasks*. This distinction helps in understanding effective teaching. By considering general *qualities* of effective teaching, and the component *tasks* involved in effective teaching, a clear framework can be designed to help planning and the effective management of learning environments. The distinction focuses on the qualities and broad aspects of teaching which appear to be important in determining its effectiveness. These include such qualities as good rapport with students, motivating and dynamic sessions, and pitching the subject knowledge and expected work output at an appropriate level of difficulty. Tasks refer to the activities and practices involved in teaching, such as planning a session or assessing students' progress. These elements are interrelated; however, the search for *qualities* is explicitly judgemental in character and may cut across a number of different *tasks* involved in teaching.

Creating and maintaining a good/positive learning environment

The creation of a positive learning environment is a key aspect that influences the motivation of students, and facilitates a positive attitude towards their learning. In terms of teaching skills, creating a purposeful learning environment means that the tutor should not only be well organised and well prepared, but start sessions on time, keep sessions running smoothly and monitor students' work and progress. It is the acceptance by the students of the tutor's organisation and management of tasks, as well as their willingness to produce a positive effort in relation to the task, that characterises a purposeful and task-orientated environment. The tutor who establishes challenging yet realistic opportunities for success within the sessions facilitates this positive orientation; it also gives the learner the opportunity to build self-esteem through a productive, constructive and supportive experience. Once again it is the tutor who is the catalyst for this in terms of planning motivating, stimulating and appropriately pitched levels of subject knowledge that will create a meaningful experience.

Relationships

The types of relationship tutors establish with their students will influence the learning environment. A positive climate is most likely to be achieved where there is mutual respect and rapport between the tutor and students. It is important that the tutor is able to convey a sense of understanding and value of the students' perspective on an array of issues (academic, personal and social).

Monitoring the learning environment

Regardless of the fact that a tutor may establish clear, challenging and reasonable tasks, there will be students who work to negotiate the boundaries of tutor expectations with a view to expanding their own terms. In an attempt to maintain the necessary 'dominance' in the relationship a tutor needs to monitor what the students are doing and to assess their compliance with the task. Students are expected to be accountable for their work and to adhere to the expectations of the tutor, but the tutor needs to monitor the learning environment in order to determine this. Effective monitoring of a session, whether a lecture or practical, is achieved through good movement around the class and effective positioning. It is essential that the tutor circulate around the class in such a way that they are able to see the entire group. This usually demands a variety of strategies, depending on the nature and context of the mode of delivery of the session. By keeping the whole group in view, a tutor is able to interact on a number of levels with individuals, pairs and small groups as well as the whole group.

Reflection and evaluation

Reflection and evaluation should form a continuous cycle underlying the tutor's decision-making process. Chapter 7 gives a detailed account of critical reflection for improving pedagogic practice. However, no planning and preparation is complete without an evaluation of the product. This can happen at two levels. An immediate response to your own endeavours may be recorded at the end of a session. This will give you a 'gut' reaction that you can critically reflect on at a later date in conjunction with further evidence gathered from student evaluations.

The second level requires a critique from you in relation to student comments and your own perceptions. This critique should answer questions such as what were the problems and how can they be addressed in the future and why did these problems or issues arise, and what can I learn from them? The results of such reflection should be fed into future planning and preparation. Thus the cycle demonstrated in Figure 4.1 continues.

Concluding comments

Planning and preparation are the key elements of effective teaching. This chapter has put forward a variety of ways in which planning can take place. A proforma has been designed to assist in the planning of sessions. This is not a definitive template but a tool to assist in the development of teaching sessions. A well-planned session will always have the potential of being a good teaching and learning session. At the very least it will be more effective than an unplanned session.

Chapter 5

Programme and course design

Introduction

Programme development and design is more important than just content for a course of study. It is important to understand and realise that the programme development process involves more than just the separate components of the programme (i.e. that of aims, objectives, learning outcomes, content, learning, assessment and evaluation). Understanding the interrelationships between these components is key to good practice. If the interrelationships are not considered there is a danger that course aims will not be assessed, that teaching can become relatively inefficient and unfocused and that student learning is accompanied by frustration and underachievement.

In this first section of this chapter I consider and illustrate the relationships between the components of the programme development process, so that the various parts of the process can be co-ordinated to bring about effective changes to a teaching programme. The illustrations will also help in the culmination of evidence for a portfolio suitable for ILT accreditation.

Curriculum and programme development: the changing context

Programme and course development and particularly curriculum development in higher education is increasingly being influenced by external factors such as the demands of the Quality Assurance Agency (QAA) and Subject Review. These external demands have required academics to use such terms as aims, learning outcomes, and assessment tools and evaluation models. To be effective, curriculum development and thus course or programme development must have a sound theoretical basis. There must be a structure to the programme or course that enables decisions to be made related to the nature and quality of the learning that is to take place. There must also be a model for the development, which draws together the various aspects of the programme or course development. These must include aspects such as learning outcomes and assessment. However, in order for such terminology to be used effectively there is a need to consider the types of questions academic teachers need to ask in order to develop a model that will help design a programme or course.

Below, I show how a model for a programme or course development can be built up based on the types of question an academic teacher needs to engage in if they are to develop a quality programme of learning and teaching.

I Developing a model for programme and course design

In the past, most university courses and programmes used a very simple model of development such as identify content and assess it (Figure 5.1). This form still exists but cannot be perceived as good practice. This simplistic model demonstrates the commonly held view in higher education that education merely consists of facts which have to be assessed, often through formal examination. This model makes some fundamental assumptions related to higher education at all levels. These include:

- The ability to pass examinations is the best method for assessing student selection and performance.
- Knowledge is the accumulation of brick upon brick of content and information (Rogers, 1969).

This simple model, based on the assumptions indicated above is very limiting and inadequate, but it does allow academic teachers to ask two fundamental but basic questions in relation to developing a programme or course for their students. These are:

1 Why am I teaching this content?
2 How do I know how successful I have been?

These questions may be interpreted as dealing with content (Question 1) and indirectly with assessment (Question 2). But how does this help the academic teacher who wishes to enable students to learn? The model is very basic, but by answering the questions the academic teacher has to question the validity and significance of what is being taught, the possible need to balance breadth and depth, and the relevance and interest of the content to the students. However, what this model ignores is that all students do not learn in the same way, nor does it take account of the differing learning

Figure 5.1 A simple model of development

environments that may assist learning to take place. The model also gives no indication as to the sequencing of content, and the possible hierarchical structure and nature of some forms of knowledge. The model also fails to show how concepts are linked, or indeed if there are any unifying concepts or strands to the development of the curriculum or programme.

Good practice requires the developer of a programme or course to consider the above issues. In order to do this they need to ask themselves a series of questions, including:

1   Why am I teaching this in a particular way?
2   How should I organise the content of my course/programme or curriculum?

If these questions are asked the model may be slightly improved, and be perceived as shown in Figure 5.2. This model still neglects essential elements that will promote planning for effective learning, such as what are the aims of the programme, how will student learning outcomes be monitored or assessed, what implications does the programme have for resources, etc.? To improve this model further, the academic teacher has to ask additional questions related to what needs to be taught, how it is to be taught and the purpose for teaching the selected content.

The questions that should now be asked are:

1   What are the aims of the programme or curriculum?
2   What are the learning outcomes of the programme? By this I mean, what do I expect my students to be able to do at the end of the programme?
3   How will I know whether these outcomes have been attained?
4   How and what type of information technology (IT) will be appropriate for this programme?
5   What resources should be used for this programme?

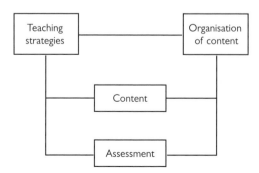

Figure 5.2 Improved model

This model is now much more sophisticated and can be used to plan a programme, singular course or module. The crucial element in this more sophisticated model is the question relating to aims and learning outcomes. Programmes, courses or singular modules all need their aims to be central. Figure 5.3 shows that teaching, course content, its organisation and the assessment that goes with it rely heavily on clearly formulated aims and learning outcomes. A further important element is missing from this model: evaluation. I will return to this component later. We now need to consider the programme development process.

2 The process of designing a curriculum or programme

Many curriculum development models have been put forward over the years, but in essence all have some generic elements and basic requirements. The various models have evolved through asking some key questions in relation to what needs to be learned and taught. When you are developing a curriculum, programme, course or module it is advisable to ask the following questions prior to planning and developing the course:

- What educational purpose is this course serving?
- What learning experience can be provided by the course as a means of attaining the above purpose?
- How can I effectively organise and manage these learning experiences?
- How can I determine whether the purposes are being attained?

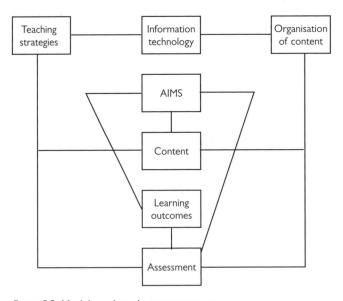

Figure 5.3 Model used to plan a programme

Although these questions may at first appear theoretical and complex, they may be further broken down to help the process of developing the curriculum or programme. This process may be viewed as five phases:

1 The selection of aims and learning outcomes.
2 The selection of learning experiences that will help in the attainment of aims and learning outcomes.
3 The selection of content (subject matter) through which the aims and learning outcomes may be attained.
4 The organisation and integration of content to learning experiences and teaching–learning strategies.
5 Evaluation of the effectiveness of the aims to the learning outcomes achieved by the students.

Simplified again, this can be translated to:

1 Aims.
2 Learning outcomes.
3 Content.
4 Assessment.
5 Evaluation.
6 Feedback.

This suggests that programme or course development progresses in a linear fashion. This of course is not always the case. However, the above model does provide a working scenario for development. The academic teacher needs to consider the assumptions under which the above model operates so that other elements may be considered when planning a programme.

The above assumes that many aims and learning outcomes can be specified at the beginning of a programme. Although many can, often new and unexpected aims or learning outcomes develop as the course is taught. It is for this reason that all elements of a programme be continually evaluated. Second, it assumes that all aims and learning outcomes can be assessed. This too is not always the case. As you will see in Chapter 7, assessment clearly demonstrates how and why it should be used within learning and teaching contexts. Content is a main area for consideration, as this can determine the aims of the programme as well as its learning outcomes. However, content must not drive the programme course or module. Content must be viewed as a vehicle for learning and is closely linked to the aims and learning outcomes of the designed course.

Figure 5.4 shows how the model may be viewed and used as a tool for development. This starts to connect the programme or course learning outcomes to the learning experiences required by the students, as well as the

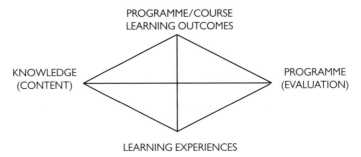

Figure 5.4 The model as a tool for development

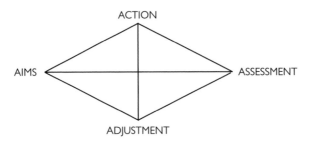

Figure 5.5 Cyclical development and improvement of the model

knowledge base on which those learning outcomes may be assessed. Taking the model one step further requires the academic teacher to think in a cyclical manner, so that the programme may be continually developed and improved. This is demonstrated in Figure 5.5. When a new programme, course or module is being developed the academic teacher will have goals and hopes related to the programme, course or module. These are key motivational factors in its development and cannot be dismissed from the process.

Goals and hopes make the development process real. These can be viewed as a good starting point for development. Figure 5.6 shows how individual hopes and goals fit into the development cycle. Goals are taken to be the general outcomes a course of study might wish to attain. Many of these goals are turned into specific detailed aims of the course. Generally these more specific aims will be assessed; by that I mean how successfully have the students achieved the course aims? Evaluation covers the efficacy of teaching, feedback from the students, and the assessment procedures against the learning outcomes of the course.

Points for consideration

Using the programme development model above, consider the following issues in relation to a course or module you are in the process of developing or about to develop.

- How has this module or course been developed in the past?
- How do I normally plan a course or module?
- Does my approach consider all aspects of programme development?
- How effective is my approach to planning and developing a course?
- Have I taken account of student learning?

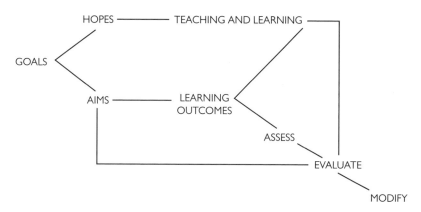

Figure 5.6 Individual hopes and goals in the development cycle

Developing course aims and learning outcomes

Teaching is aimed at helping students learn something they had previously not known; hence when designing and developing a course it is necessary to consider how the student will learn and the changes in their thinking that are needed to help the learning process. Making teaching/learning intentions explicit is both helpful to the student and to the teacher. This approach is often referred to as outcomes-based learning and planning. The use of learning outcomes is now dominating the higher education literature and is based on the recommendations of the Dearing Report (NCIHE, 1997). This report was explicit in its requirements for higher education to develop programme specifications. Outcomes are viewed as a middle ground between statements of learning which are considered to be over-generalised (learning aims) and those which are over-specified (learning objectives) (Walker, 1994). Despite the debates that continue with respect to learning outcomes, learning object-ives, aims, etc., academic teachers have to deal with them and include them in any future course development. Pedagogically, learning outcomes are a useful tool. They are used to make explicit to those who are to teach the programme, as well as those who are to learn from the programme, what is expected and what should be the achievable outcomes of the programme.

When aims and learning outcomes are being selected, the academic teacher must take account of a number of issues related to their students, the staff going to teach the programme or course, the resource implications of the programme and the nature of the subject being taught. Each has its own fundamental implication for the course aims and learning outcomes.

Points for consideration

Use the questions below in relation to a course or module you are in the process of developing, or about to develop, as a way of establishing the possible framework for its development.

- How does this course intend to develop the students?
- How will the nature of the subject to be taught influence the content of the programme?
- How does the course take account of external demands, such as industry or accrediting bodies?
- What economic and resource restraints will the programme have?
- Can the programme be staffed by appropriately qualified academics?

At the outset of development these factors cannot be ignored. If a programme is developed without such consideration it may well produce a course of study that is irrelevant to students and cannot be staffed.

Syllabi, content and understanding

New programmes, courses or modules in higher education are usually developed to meet a changing need within the subject area itself or from external pressures such as industry or accrediting bodies such as the English Nursing Board (ENB), Institute for Professional Development (IPD), or the Institute of Physics (IoP). Development reflects the need to change. This change is intended for students to learn new information, knowledge, skills, etc. Key to development is understanding what changes in learning are required by the students. Contents of programmes are traditionally communicated by syllabi. The introduction to thermodynamics, evidence-based practice, the theories of Karl Marx and the works of Shakespeare are all examples of potential course content as frequently expressed in university documentation. When content is set out as a syllabus it is easy to obscure the range of theories, concepts, principles, processes, skills and techniques that students are expected to learn and teachers are equally expected to cover. Any new course should aim to change the way students think about issues, concepts, facts and principles. To do this, students need to be able to change their conceptions. This is very difficult to do, and there is much literature to demonstrate how resilient individuals' prior conceptions are. Hence any new course development must ask the following questions:

- What changes in understanding are expected from students undergoing this programme or course?
- What will the students be able to do as a result of following this programme?
- What will students be able to do as a result of these changes after they complete the course that they could not do before?

The above questions are key to selecting programme or course aims and learning outcomes. Writing aims and learning outcomes, and thinking systematically about what students need to understand and how they will understand them, is essential to successful programme and course planning. Use the points for consideration given below to help you derive the nature and context of the understanding you wish your students to be engaged in.

Points for consideration

Using the above questions, identify the key elements such as concepts, processes and theories that you think the course you are developing requires. Use this information to answer the following:

- What do I want my students to understand?
- Why is this understanding important?
- What should this understanding enable them to do?
- How can I establish whether or not they have understood?

Selecting aims and learning outcomes

Selecting aims and learning outcomes is a means to changing student learning and the experience in which that change will occur. Aims can be thought of as general statements of educational intent; as seen from an external point of view they give a programme or course a destination, while learning outcomes are more specific, and concentrate on what students are expected to learn and demonstrate that they have learned. Any programme should give a clear indication as to what it hopes to achieve so that students know whether or not they want to achieve those things on offer, and therefore enrol on the programme. In this way teaching and learning can be directed to achieving the stated aims and the most appropriate assessment procedures chosen to establish whether those aims have been achieved.

Aims can be selected from a variety of sources, the most common of which are the subject matter itself, external agencies and the constraint of teaching staff.

Subject matter

Deriving aims from subject matter requires the academic teacher to ask the question: what makes that subject distinctive? For example, certain skills can only be taught in dentistry, certain ways of viewing the particulate nature of matter can only be taught in chemistry, and certain logic and problem solving can only be taught in law, and so on. It is these distinctive features which should be used in deriving aims from subject matter. Equally important are the types of aims that are common to groups of subjects (e.g. the ability to search literature and the ability to communicate).

Points for consideration

Using the subject/topic area that requires development, consider and identify the particular aspects that are key to the subject and how these may be turned into aims for your programme or course.

Classifying aims as a means to identifying learning outcomes

Aims may be classified in a variety of ways. Educational literature regarding the pros and cons of classifying aims is widespread (Bloom, 1964; Gagné, 1967; Kibler, 1970; McGaghie, 1974). Although much of this literature is old it still holds today. How the classifications are used and interpreted are again open to discussion. The aim here is to introduce the levels of classification as a tool for identifying learning outcomes.

There are three main areas of classification derived from Bloom (1964). These include cognitive, affective and psychomotor aims, and these can roughly be interpreted as knowing, feeling and doing. Cognitive elements include knowledge, comprehension, application, analysis synthesis and evaluation. Affective elements include receiving, responding, valuing, organisation and characterisation. The psychomotor elements include initiatory pre-routine and routinised behaviour.

The literature suggests that these should to be both hierarchical and cumulative. This classification can be further broken down to help the process of the selection of aims and learning outcomes as follows:

1   Using Gagné's (1967) approach, learning can be thought of as:

    - recall;
    - concept learning;
    - generalisation learning;
    - problem solving.

2   A possible approach to learning in medicine might include:

    - information gathering;
    - problem solving;
    - clinical judgement;
    - relationship to patients;
    - continuing responsibility;
    - emergency care;
    - relationship with colleagues;
    - professional values;
    - overall competence.

3   In physics, course learning might be thought of as:

    - collection of information;
    - application of the principles of physics;
    - application of mathematical techniques;
    - application of experimental techniques;
    - flexibility in problem solving;
    - evaluation in problem solving;
    - interpretation and explanation.

Classifications such as those given above are a good starting point for selecting more specific aims for your own programme. When writing your aims consider the following tips:

- Lower cognitive skills include recall of information and basic understanding of concepts.
- Acquisition of information includes using references.
- Higher cognitive skills include ability to generalise, evaluate, depth of thought, critical analysis, problem solving, originality.
- Study skills include skills in preparation, seeking information, and thought communication, both verbal and written.

- Practical skills include clinical skills and experimental design and techniques.
- Team work.

Combination of one of the higher order cognitive skills (e.g. problem solving and practical skills) might produce the following aims within a science subject. At the end of this programme students will be able to:

- manipulate laboratory equipment;
- recognise when adequate results have been obtained;
- discover errors and be able to correct them;
- evaluate the accuracy of the experiment.

In a law programme the combination of higher cognitive problem solving and practical skills might produce the following aims. At the end of the programme students will be able to:

- Understand and be able to identify, use and evaluate rules, concepts and principles of law, their derivation, and various theories that attempt to systematise them.
- Acquire the techniques of legal reasoning and argument, in oral and written form.

In an English literature programme the combination of higher cognitive critical analysis skills and practical skills might produce the following aims. At the end of the programme students will be able to:

- Read broadly in English, American and world literature.
- Understand in depth the literary works which are covered by the programme.
- Respond to literature both affectively and evaluatively.
- Use critical skills in reading unfamiliar texts.

Points for consideration

Using the above classification and examples, identify and specify the aims of your intended programme, course or module.

Learning outcomes

Chapter 3 dealt with theories of learning and their implications for good practice. Much of the discussion rested on deep and surface learning. Here we return to these two notions as they relate to selecting learning outcomes for a programme of study, course or module.

In the classifications of aims the cognitive domain of learning suggested that understanding covered six levels, the lowest being factual knowledge and the highest being evaluation of information. This taxonomy, although criticised, has been extended over the years and has been systematically used to develop programmes of learning. Most recently the discussion has moved towards levels of learning outcomes. The Dearing Report (NCIHE, 1997, Recommendation 21) suggests four domains of intended learning outcomes specifically for programmes of study in higher education within the United Kingdom. These are:

1   Knowledge and understanding;
2   Key skills (e.g. communication, numeracy, IT, learning to learn);
3   Cognitive skills (e.g. ability in critical analysis);
4   Subject-specific skills (e.g. laboratory skills, clinical skills).

The above areas can both reassure and cause concern for institutions of higher education. Some schools or faculties are already using learning outcomes that fit the above frameworks while others are not. It is important to understand the levels of learning students engage in as well as how these levels can be translated effectively into levels of learning outcomes. It is these levels of outcome that are needed for developing a programme, course or module.

The work of Biggs (1987, 1989) on deep and surface learning is most useful to consider here as a tool for developing levels of learning outcomes. Biggs suggests that there are five levels of learning, which can be expressed as:

1   An increase in knowledge;
2   Memorising;
3   The acquisition of procedures;
4   The abstraction of meaning;
5   Understanding reality.

He surmised that the first three levels concentrate on surface approaches to learning, and the last two levels required deep approaches to learning. These differing levels relate to perceptions about content and teaching. One must appreciate that there is a difference between knowing facts or understanding concepts and the different approaches. Ramsden (1992, p. 45) suggests that:

An approach is not about learning facts versus learning concepts: it is about learning *just* the unrelated facts (or procedures) versus learning facts *in relation to* concepts. Surface is, at best, about quantity without quality; deep is about quality and quantity.

Biggs (1989, p. 10) wrote:

> Knowing facts and how to carry out operations may well be part of the
> means for understanding and interpreting the world, but the qualitative
> conception stops at the facts and skills. A quantitative change in know-
> ledge does not in itself change understanding. Rote learning scientific
> formulae may be one of the things scientists do, but it is not the way
> scientists think.

The implication for selecting levels of learning outcomes from Biggs' and
Ramsden's arguments is that the type of learning students will engage in
depends on the level of meaning students place on the knowledge that they
are expected to acquire.

To achieve effective learning outcomes it is important not to restate the
syllabus topics using the vocabulary of aims and learning outcomes. The
following are examples of how *not* to write learning outcomes:

1   A lecture or session topic in chemistry may be rates of reactions; the
    learning outcome then becomes 'To acquire the knowledge about rates
    of reactions'.
2   A lecture or session in English literature may be Shakespeare sonnets;
    the learning outcome then becomes 'To acquire knowledge and
    understanding about Shakespeare sonnets'.

Both of these examples highlight the basic failure of merely interpreting
syllabus content into learning outcomes. First, the learning outcomes give
very little information to the students as to what is expected of them and
how they should go about achieving the set learning outcomes. Second, the
language in which they are written gives no insight into expectations. What
does it mean to acquire knowledge and understanding about rates of reactions or Shakespeare sonnets? One assumes that students will be required to
understand the key concepts related to rates of reactions or Shakespeare
sonnets and how these concepts can be related to real situations (e.g.
unknown reactions and new poetry).

These two examples could be rewritten to clearly show the expectations
of the learning that students should be engaged in:

1   'To explain the meaning and function of rates of reaction in relation to
    the concept of equilibrium', and 'To explain the significance of rates of
    reaction within the context of thermal dissociation'.
2   'To explain the meaning and function of sonnets in relation to Shake-
    speare writing', and 'To explain the significance of sonnets within the
    context of contemporary poetry'.

Students may not know what all these terms mean at the start of their programme or course, but it will help direct their learning to the relevant literature, as well as helping them to review their knowledge of the topic as they proceed through the programme or course. The purpose of learning outcomes is not only to help the student attain the aims of the programme but also to help those who teach the programme to provide a systematic and coherent course for the student. Each level of learning outcome can be associated with words and phrases that depict expectations. To assist the process further, Bloom's taxonomy shows how levels of learning can be used to select and derive levels of learning outcomes. For example, knowledge may be viewed as names, recall, definitions, lists, records and stating facts. Explanation, description, discussion and recognition may exemplify comprehension. Application may be shown by illustration, application of facts and information, demonstration and practical skills. Analysis is exemplified by calculation, the ability to distinguish sets of data, analysis of information and data and the interpretation of tests. Synthesis with Bloom's taxonomy represents the formulation of ideas and hypotheses, organisation of information and data and the ability to propose design and creative thinking. Finally, evaluation is considered to be the ability to appraise, evaluate, compare and assess situations and information.

Points for consideration

Using the above examples from Bloom's taxonomy, select and derive the levels of learning outcomes for the programme, course or module you are developing.

Aims, learning outcomes and teaching

Establishing your aims and learning outcomes is the first step to developing a systematic programme or course. There are, however, other elements that now need to be considered. These include the nature and context of assessment, as well as the possible teaching strategies that may be deployed. Programme design has illustrated how aims are linked to content, the way content is taught, organised and assessed. However, unless teaching is planned to achieve programme, course or module aims, then these aims will most likely not be achieved. This may appear to be an obvious statement, but consider the following situation. Undergraduates are often criticised for not being able to reference correctly, or to use reference material. Yet often the use of the library comes high in course aims. What this demonstrates is that if that aim is not achieved, if teaching and learning experiences are not devised early in the course to provide the necessary experiences, students will not be able to demonstrate their assumed learning outcomes.

The most useful way around this problem is to state the aims in terms of what the student is expected to do. In this way there is a clear indication as to what teaching and learning has to take place in order for the aims to be achieved. Sequencing of topics can occur systematically once aims and learning outcomes have been selected. The main focus for sequencing topics is to allow students to progress through their learning in a coherent and systematic way. It also allows for those teaching the course to know what has been taught before their contribution and what might follow their own. Thus, to give consistency to the students' learning, the following basic principles for selecting learning experiences should be considered:

1   Sequencing of a course should focus on the aims for student learning.
2   Students must be given sufficient experiences to enable aims to be attained.
3   Topics should follow systematically so that students can develop their conceptual thinking in a coherent way.
4   Teaching should be organised to assist student learning; this can be facilitated so that staff are aware of what is being taught, and when.
5   The same learning experience can bring about several different outcomes.

Case studies of effective course design

It is always difficult to imagine how theory becomes practice. Below are some case studies of effective course design. They aim to be exemplars, but must be seen as particular to the courses being discussed. Each approach may be modified to suit the purpose. What is important in all these case studies is the understanding of how teaching and learning are represented. Good courses make their expectations clear, but they also allow freedom and provide structure. All the case studies are based on unpublished material using fictitious names.

1   Designing a course for the management of change: Julie Green.
2   The aims and content of a chemistry course for chemical engineers.
3   Making the aims of a research methods programme explicit.
4   A problem based nursing course.

Problem-based learning is increasingly coming to the forefront of medical education. In some institutions it is the main pedagogical approach to teaching and learning. Boud and Feletti (1996) reviewed the range and variety of problem-based learning and found the following characteristics to be generic in most courses:

•   Integration of disciplinary and clinical and non-clinical subject matter.

- A non-didactic facilitator.
- Students, and not the teacher, make decisions about what they need to learn in relation to the scenario set by the problem.
- Small groups of students explore a problem in a structured way so that knowledge and understanding is shared.
- Synthesis and test of information; students report back on findings.
- Formulate learning questions.

In principle, problem-based courses focus on the types of problems that are typically found in professional life. The main requirements for such programmes are that students have to identify the nature and context of the problem and the information they require to tackle and solve the problem. In this type of course knowledge, skills and professional attitudes are addressed simultaneously.

The following course was designed to enable post-registration nurses to tackle questions related to diagnostic and problem-based skills and issues which were thought to be essential for post-registration work. The first step towards establishing the course aims was a realisation that the participants of the course would require content that helped develop professional skills. But at the same time, and more importantly, the participants were able to problem solve while understanding the content knowledge they would be dealing with. The aims of the programme were stated as follows:

1   To develop skills of critical analysis, particularly in relation to proposed solutions to problems.
2   To develop skills of information collection and analysis.
3   To develop an appreciation of how to problem solve.
4   To develop an understanding for alternative solutions.
5   To be introduced to a variety of standard methods of analysis.
6   To develop independent study skills.

Following these aims, specific learning outcomes were developed to guide both teacher and student to understand the requirements of the programme. Included in the learning outcomes were knowledge, clinical problem solving and professional values.

Aims and assessment

Assessment is a key element of higher education. A major function of assessment is to provide feedback to students and staff on how well the course aims have been achieved. This requires the assessment procedures of the programme to be valid and reliable. Assessment procedures have to have a high content validity. Assessment is dealt with in greater detail in

Chapter 6. However, for the purpose of this section a brief discussion related to reliability and validity is required as a means of understanding the links between programme aims and assessment requirements.

Reliability and validity are terms used commonly in assessment. Four types of validity are recognised:

1   Content validity (is the content covered?);
2   Predictive validity (can the assessment achievement predict future performance?);
3   Concurrent validity (is an aim being assessed in more than one way?);
4   Construct validity (does this indirect method of assessment tell us if an aim has been achieved?)

Reliability indicates the consistency with which an assessment procedure measures the aim(s) it is supposed to be measuring.

An assessment procedure can be highly reliable but have a low content validity. For example, the achievement of certain skills might be a course aim. A multiple-choice test paper of high reliability could be used as a sole form of assessment for that course, but as far as assessing skills are concerned, that test could have no content validity. The practical implication of this is that if assessment procedures do not reflect all the course aims (i.e. if they do not have high content validity) then the aims which are not assessed will more than likely not be achieved by the students.

Points for consideration

Within the programme, course or modules you are developing state the aims of the programme, then using the questions below identify the nature of the assessment appropriate to the programme.

- What are the aims of the programme?
- What learning experiences do the students need to achieve the stated aims?
- What type of assessment best fits the learning experiences?
- What type of assessment tool will show content validity and be reliable?

As a final consideration point, here are four key questions to guide your design and development of a programme, course or module.

> **Points for consideration**
>
> * What do I want my students to learn?
> * How do should I organise the teaching and learning experience?
> * How should I assess the learning that has taken place?
> * How can I establish the effectiveness of the course in relation to the learning outcomes?

Evaluating the programme or course

Evaluating and reviewing your programme or course is essential in establishing whether key course or programme aims and objectives/learning outcomes have been met and how successfully these have been met. The first distinction to be made is that review and evaluation are not the same process, nor are they used in the same way in terms of development of a programme or course. However, both are as important as each other, when it comes to collecting evidence of course development and delivery.

Programme or course review

Individual review of a course or programme should be happening most of the time from an individual perspective. By this I mean that after each session, whether taught by you or by another member of staff, that session should be reviewed quickly and efficiently for outcome. Did students understand, should there be a recap next session, should extension work be given to some more able students, is there a need for work for less able students? These are the immediate issues that individual review requires. Evidencing this is a matter of showing how you or your colleagues have responded to immediate changes required in the delivery of the session.

Evaluating a programme or course

There are various levels of evaluation, and equally there are a variety of methods that can be used to evaluate courses. Essential to effective evaluation is an understanding of what it is to evaluate and the processes by which this is done. Key questions that frame evaluation are:

* What is evaluation?
* Why evaluate?
* What is the purpose of the evaluation?
* For whom is the evaluation being conducted?
* What is being evaluated?

- When and how will the evaluation take place?
- How do you ensure evaluation data feeds back into course planning and development?

Evaluation is more than simply filling in a questionnaire at the end of a session or programme, and then doing nothing with the responses. Systematic evaluation and feedback are the key to successful teaching and learning programmes. Evaluation is the means by which you establish what is working well in a course both from a student and tutor perspective, as well as what is not so successful. Through the collection and analysis of this information, judgements can be made as to how to improve and develop the programme, course or module. *Evaluation is about gaining information that helps to make informed judgements about course effectiveness.* One of the main reasons to evaluate is to establish how well the course meets the original aims and learning outcomes, but this is not the only purpose of the evaluation. It is essential that both students and staff teaching the programme are informed as to the effective and non-effective elements of the course or programme.

Points for consideration

In relation to the programme you are currently developing, consider the following questions:

- Has the programme been evaluated before? If so, how regularly and what was done with the evaluation data?
- If the data are available are they of value in developing future evaluation tools?
- How regularly will evaluation take place and when will you evaluate?
- Will you evaluate throughout the course or just at the end of the course, or is it best to do both?
- How appropriate and user friendly are your evaluation methods?
- Are participants encouraged to use their own words in the evaluation tool?
- If the programme involves practical elements how will you evaluate against practically described learning outcomes?
- How will you disseminate and discuss the evaluation findings?
- How will you develop the course following the evaluation outcomes?

The above points are aimed at focusing the reasons for conducting evaluations of your programmes and courses. It is also to emphasise the importance of feedback of information to those concerned with the course or programme as well as taking the evidence and developing and improving the course or programme for the future.

The next stage of evaluation is deciding which elements of the course or programme are going to be evaluated and when. This is particularly important if a programme, course or module has many components and is taught by a variety of people. Evaluation should check for continuity, progression of learning, consistency of teaching, and whether the programme aims and learning outcomes as a whole are being achieved. In order to establish what should or should not be evaluated within a programme or course the following two areas should be considered:

1   Identification of broad areas for evaluation;
2   Generating specific questions for the evaluation.

1 Identification of broad areas for evaluation

The broad areas should encapsulate all areas of the programme. To make the evaluation effective and not cumbersome these may be outlined as follows:

- aims, objectives and learning outcomes;
- learning outcomes for the learners;
- assessment procedures;
- impact on staff and resources;
- programme balance between process, content and product;
- feedback and dissemination of evaluation data.

These areas focus on the main elements of a programme, course or module. Having established how these are to be evaluated, specific questions need to be asked so that relevant data can be collected.

2 Generating specific questions for the evaluation

Having identified the main areas for evaluation it is essential that specific questions are asked that will help the future development of the programme. These questions may relate to:

- the quality of the teaching experience;
- the quality of the learning environment/classroom;
- level of student motivation and attainment;
- appropriateness of academic level of the programme;
- organisation of the course, both from a student's and tutor's perspective;
- availability of equipment/resources;

- effectiveness of assessment;
- student support (e.g. tutor availability, returning of assignments, marking schedules, etc.).

The key to successful evaluation is to keep the tool for collecting the evaluation data focused and uncomplicated, yet making sure the questions are specific enough to obtain reliable data.

Points for consideration

In relation to the programme you are developing at present, consider the following questions:

- What is the purpose of the programme, course or module evaluation?
- Which are the main areas that need to be evaluated?
- Why are these the main areas?
- Who will be the recipient of the evaluation report?
- How will you disseminate the evaluation findings?
- How will you feed back the evaluation findings to the programme development cycle?

Evaluation methods that may be useful in a teaching learning context

Evaluating your programme is not just an administrative process that has to be completed. It is a very important element of ensuring effective teaching and learning. As teaching and learning are complex and interrelated events, evaluation methods and tools have to be chosen carefully and purposefully. Tables 5.1–5.3 offer some suggestions on what may be evaluated and the tools that can be used to obtain the data for the evaluation of the programme, course, module or teaching session. These are only examples of ways in which courses and programmes may be evaluated. The suggested tools are by no means exclusive. It is in the interest of the programme that the correct tools and methods are chosen.

Table 5.1 Quality of teaching and learning

Issues that need to be evaluated	Possible evaluation tool
Purpose, pace, and quality of teaching	**Observation:** Peer, student comment, external assessor, self
Quality of student activity and work	**Assessment:** By self, external examiners, course work, other tutors
Teaching/learning resources	**Interview/questionnaire:** Ask students and tutors
Programme content and academic level	**Questionnaire/assessment:** Ask students and tutors, compare aims and learning outcomes to student achievement
Quality of assessment procedures	**Mark book/exam papers, assignments:** Evidence of record-keeping and student progress
Tutor–Student relationship	**Interview/questionnaire:** Ask students, verbally and through confidential questionnaire

Table 5.2 Programme organisation

Issues that need to be evaluated	Possible evaluation tool
Planning and preparation	**Course material:** Evidence of schemes of work, course handbook, tutorial material lecture notes, student support
Staff/teaching styles and academic content	**Questionnaire:** To students, asking them to assess teaching sessions
Continuity and progression of learning	**Course handbook/questionnaire:** Ask students and to compare aims and learning outcomes
Institutional facilities used to support programme	**Questionnaire/interview:** Ask students and tutors
Reporting and tracking of student progress	**Student records/staff records:** Ensuring that tracking actually happens
Use of evaluation material	**Academic reports** from previous years

Table 5.3 Student motivation and attainment

Issues that need to be evaluated	Possible evaluation tool
Levels of attendance	**Registers**
Final success rate	**Finishing rates and retention rate**
Communication	**Questionnaire/interview:** Ask students either verbally or in writing whether they feel there has been good communication between tutors on the course and between themselves and their tutors
Student views	**Questionnaire/interview:** Ask students either verbally or in writing whether they feel their ideas have been valued and they have been given the opportunity to contribute and participate in their learning

---

Points for consideration

In relation to the programme you are currently developing, the following should be considered prior to setting out the evaluation process.

- Select the specific areas that will be evaluated within the programme.
- Select the evaluation strategies that will be adopted to give accurate data.
- Identify time points for the collection of evaluation data.
- Establish and state how dissemination of data and feedback procedures will be implemented.

Evaluation and feedback are essential within the quality assurance framework. Evaluation data are a means by which curricula can be seen to be succeeding in achieving the aims and standards set out by that curriculum. Acting on evaluation data and feedback to improve teaching/learning environments is essential in maintaining high standards.

The evaluation cycle (Figure 5.7) is there to assist the raising of standards. Often feedback is difficult to implement; if seen in a cyclical manner, it is easier to understand how courses can be systematically evaluated and improved to meet the demands of a changing student population.

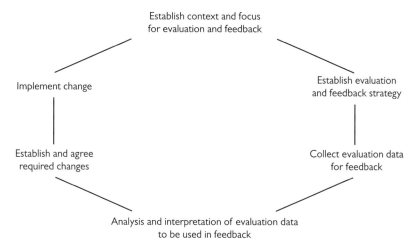

Figure 5.7 Evaluation cycle

Conclusion

This chapter has introduced the main elements of programme and course design. It has shown how programme or course aims and learning outcomes are the foundation on which a programme rests from its inception to its evaluation. Within any programme design you should be able to explain the following terms:

- aims;
- learning outcomes;
- progression;
- assessment;
- evaluation.

Programme design requires a clear understanding of the context of learning and the main areas of the subject that need to be covered by the students. How the students progress through the programme and how each element of the programme links is essential to effective course development.

Conducting teaching and learning sessions

Introduction

This chapter focuses on issues related to the management of teaching/ learning environments in higher education. It considers how effective environments may be achieved, making explicit that teaching can take many forms, and that the didactic approach is only one strategy. It reinforces the previous chapter by emphasising the need to consider class size when planning teaching and that teaching can be interactive with large groups as well as small ones. The chapter will also consider how adults learn and how these theories can be put into practice within a given session. The debate related to teaching and research in higher education and how they may be integrated into a teaching session will be considered. Research is key in all disciplines. This chapter highlights the need to see both teaching and research as integral to the learning environments of both lecturer and student.

In any teaching situation it is unlikely that the academic will have a heterogeneous group of students. It is therefore essential to understand the underlying principles of differentiated teaching and the implications this has for planning and preparation of teaching/learning material. Key to understanding differentiated learning is an appreciation that those who lecture may have different value systems about students' capabilities and aspirations to learn from the students themselves. This element needs to be recognised and addressed when teaching.

Teaching as an activity

Teaching occurs through a variety of mediums and contexts. These include lectures, tutorials, small and large group teaching, as well as lab sessions and other practically orientated learning. Key to all of these is the learning one wishes the students to engage in and what one expects students to gain from the learning experience. Choosing the appropriate learning environment requires planning, preparation and a clear notion of what is to be achieved from the session.

The lecture

> We take lecturing in higher education so much for granted that we easily
> forget just how powerful its hold is.
>
> (Ramsdens, 1992, p. 151)

Understanding the implications of the lecture
as a teaching strategy

The lecture is the standard method for teaching large classes, yet research
has shown that individuals learn better if they think about what they are
learning and that they actively engage with the information they are being
expected to learn. Comparisons between lecturers and other forms of teaching have demonstrated that where students are encouraged to discuss and
participate learning is more effective (McKeachie *et al.*, 1990). In a very
comprehensive review of the literature Bligh (1998) concluded that the
lecture was as effective as other methods as a means of transmitting information, but not more so. However, the review also stated that lectures were
less effective as a means of promoting thought, critical thinking and changing students' attitudes. Despite the research evidence, the lecture remains
the main method of information delivery and teaching strategy employed in
higher education. Bearing these comments in mind, it is essential to consider the advantages and disadvantages of the lecture as a method of
instruction.

The main reason lectures are limited in achieving learning outcomes are
related to the way individuals learn (cf. Chapter 3). Ramsden (1994, p.
167) suggests that 'active engagement, imaginative inquiry and the finding
of a suitable level are all much more likely to occur if teaching methods
that necessitate student activity, student problem-solving and question-
asking, and co-operative learning are employed'. If this is the case one
must ask why do we lecture, for on the whole the student plays a very
passive role in a lecture and is rarely engaged in active learning. The
lecture is perceived as the best way of imparting knowledge and covering
all the information students apparently need to know. However, much of
this information will be lost to students if they are passive, and effective
learning will not happen. Students need to be engaged in deep learning if
they are to develop and become autonomous, critical thinkers and
learners.

Below is a summary of the advantages and disadvantages associated with
lecturing.

Advantages

- They are an economical way of using staff time.
- Lecturers can be inspirational.
- Some lectures can save students' time by summarising a field of study.
- They can provide an up-to-date view of the subject.
- They are a good means of introducing a subject.
- Lectures provide a means of pacing a student's rate of working.

Disadvantages

- Lectures are relatively ineffective in stimulating thought.
- Lectures are relatively ineffective in stimulating changing attitudes.
- Lectures are less popular with students than other methods.
- Personal and social adjustments should not normally be the major objective of lectures.

It is generally agreed that an uninterrupted fifty-minute lecture is a poor method of learning; there is usually no student participation, no rehearsal of what is learned and no feedback to the lecturer. There is a sharp decline in student performance (expressed as the ability to recall information) as the lecturer proceeds. For example, in one study students were able to recall 70 per cent of the content of the first ten minutes of a lecture but could only recall 20 per cent of the last ten minutes (Bligh, 1998; Brown and Atkins, 1988).

If there is not an immediate application of what is imparted during a lecture then over a period of a few days there is a rapid drop in the percentage of material retained. Other factors can also aid the remembering of information given in a lecture. These include the meaningfulness of what is taught, the logical argument of presented subject matter, repetition to consolidate learning, and feedback to students on their performance in (for example) written exercises. Students appear to like to know the aims of a course of lectures. The availability of objectives is found to facilitate learning in certain instances, although the generalisability of these instances is not easily determined.

The lecturer

Students have very clear expectations of lecturers, particularly in the role of giving a lecture. High on their list is:

Clarity of presentation

- Presents material clearly and logically.
- Enables students to understand the basic principles of the subject.
- Can be clearly heard.
- Makes material intelligibly meaningful.
- Adequately covers the ground in the lecture course.
- Maintains continuity in the course.
- Adopts an appropriate pace in lectures.

Scholarship

- Shows an expert knowledge of subject.
- Illustrates practical applications of the theory of subject.
- Refers to latest developments in subject.
- Makes links between theory and practice.

Willingness to develop students

- Readily considers students' viewpoints.
- Allows questions during lectures.
- Stimulates students to think independently and critically.

The above elements are used as an illustration of what students find facilitative and non-facilitative in lectures. It is essential to consider student learning and engagement when constructing and delivering a lecture.

Points for consideration

The following points are the most commonly sited reasons for student dissatisfaction with lectures. Consider these points and ways in which they may be avoided.

- Lecturer incoherent.
- Lecturer gave too much or too little detail and failed to emphasise main points.
- Lecturer failed to come down to students' level.
- Lecturer spoke badly.
- It was very difficult for students to take notes.
- Lecturer was dull or uninspiring because he/she merely read notes.
- Lecturer's writing and diagrams were too small and inappropriate.

Preparing for a lecture

The following questions should be answered before preparing for a lecture.

- What aims do I have in mind? (See Chapter 5)
- Is the lecture method the best teaching technique for achieving these aims?
- What kind of lecture should be given?
- What generalisations do I wish to convey?
- How can I best organise the material?
- What audio-visual aids will be useful?
- What student preparation and follow-up activities are planned?

If, as research shows, that student achievement drops dramatically as the lecture proceeds, ways should be found to re-motivate the students throughout the lecture. This can be done in a variety of ways, including:

- Asking questions throughout the lecture.
- Placing students in small groups to discuss a given problem for a short period of time.
- Encouraging student problem solving on board.
- Actively engaging students throughout the lecture.

The above suggestions are also a way by which students can immediately apply the knowledge they are being taught. This will enhance the retention rate of knowledge for the students.

Types of lecture

The lecture can be and is often thought of as a single entity. However, this is not the case, and it is helpful to planning if the lecture can be seen as having several alternative approaches. Lectures can have different foci; these include:

- *Information and facts*: The focus here is on the giving of information in either formal or informal ways. Students tend to be more passive, but lecturers can make information giving stimulating with effort and preparation.
- *Problem solving*: The problem-centred lecture consists of the lecturer asking a question or posing a problem and then presenting relevant information in the arguments. The focus of the lecture is the problem.
- *Activity*: The activity approach lecture is one where students are actively involved by actually conducting some form of activity during the course of the lecture, such as trying to write a short poem in a particular style,

taking part in a demonstration, role play or simulation of a particular phenomenon.

- *Issue*: The main focus here is that a lecture concentrates on a significant issue. All tasks, activities or problems are related to that issue. The aim is to make students aware of the issues at hand through a variety of perspectives.

Organising the lecture

If the lecture is the best method of delivery to achieve the aims that you have in mind, and when the type of presentation has been decided upon, the next stage is to organise the material. This can be done in four stages.

1 Write down what you hope to achieve as a result of the lecture.
2 Write down the key points (i.e. the major generalisations).
3 Arrange the key points into the most logical order of presentation.
4 Make your lecture cohesive for the students.

Lecturers are most effective when the lecturer uses brief notes consisting of headings and sub-headings rather than full notes which are read or copied on to a board, overhead projector screen or computer screen. If notes are planned and presented in a logical order it makes student learning more engaging. However, part of organising the lecture must also concern itself with the resources the students are going to be given in relation to the lecture. For example, are the students going to be given handouts? If so what will the handouts consist of?

It is important to consider the learning that is expected from the lecture. Thus the extra material given to the students should not only consolidate the lecture but extend the interaction with the knowledge given. Handouts might contain a list of learning objectives, a summary of the lecture, useful references, diagrams, and questions to be answered or further researched. Handouts are not only an extension of the lecture but can be seen to be another way of engaging students in autonomous learning.

Delivering a lecture

Planning and preparation by lecturers has been stressed as a means to successful delivery of lectures. When delivering the lecture bear in mind the following points:

- Do not include too much material in the lecture.
- Organise the lecture so that students can follow your progress through the concepts, problems or issues being addressed in the lecture. This can be achieved by subdividing the topic under a number of main headings

and presenting the headings on an OHP or PowerPoint presentation at the start of the lecture. This will facilitate the students' appreciation of the structure and framework of the overall lecture.

- Do not work too quickly. Remember that what comes easily to you may be the first time the students have encountered the problems or issues you are introducing or discussing. A major failure of the lecture is the assumption that students can follow and keep up with the lecturer. It is the responsibility of the lecturer to ensure that learning is taking place.
- Use your lecture notes as reminders; do not dictate them to the students, as this is a waste of time. It is better to photocopy notes than dictate. Use the time to explain, expand and engage the students in the information you are trying to impart.
- Appear confident when talking to your students. Look directly at them rather than the ceiling, etc. and walk around the lecture room. Do not stay behind the lectern or desk as this appears defensive to the students.
- Constantly try to assess how the students are responding to your lecture and react accordingly. This may well mean that you change direction in the lecture. Ask the students if there are points that need clarification, etc. This will help gain the support and engagement of the students.

Although there are no hard and fast rules that guide a good, well-planned and delivered lecture, the following general plan is worth considering:

- A good introduction to the lecture, specifying aims and learning outcomes to be achieved.
- Distribution of handouts.
- An overview of the lecture (important generalisations are given).
- Small breaks revolving around specific activities (discussion with other students concerning a particular problem, or individualised problem-solving task, etc.).
- A summary of all salient points, and general points revised and reinforced.

Points for consideration

Using the above suggestions, consider and create a framework for lecture design based on your discipline. The purpose of the framework is to help speed the planning and preparation of your lectures.

Below are some suggestions for making lecturing more effective. These should help particularly if you bear in mind the following quote from Professor Gibbsons (electrical engineering):

When you start teaching and you're dealing with undergraduates, and you look out there and you see that confused look, the chances are that the context isn't there. Because if the context is there, [students] can follow all kinds of arguments, if they see roughly where you're going.

(p. 131)

Checklist for effective lecturing

Be prepared

- Outline clear objectives of your lecture. An objective should not be 'to cover material'. An objective is why the material is important.
- Develop an outline; create effective visuals for the main points.
- Limit the main points in a lecture to between three and five.
- Do not use lecture time to reiterate readings. Refer to them and highlight key points.
- Plan for diverse learners. Use verbal, visual and physical (hands-on exercises, simulations) approaches.
- If you are nervous, write out the first two or three minutes of the lecture.

Engage your audience

- Focus attention early on using quotes, a snappy visual, an anecdote, or other appropriate material relevant to the topic.
- Share your outline. Emphasise your objectives and key points in the beginning, as you get to them and as a summary at the end.
- Integrate visuals, multi-media, discussion and small group techniques.
- Link information to students' prior knowledge (i.e. common experiences or previous course work).
- Exhibit enthusiasm for the topic and information. Remember that you are modelling your discipline.
- Give students time to think, and genuine opportunities to respond.

Get feedback

- Observe students' non-verbal communication: note taking, response to questions, eye contact, seating patterns, response to humour. Are they 'with' you?
- Ask students to respond in one or two sentences to the three following questions:

    1   What stood out as most important in today's lecture?
    2   What are you confused about?
    3   Ask students for their comments/suggestions.

Suggestions from a variety of disciplines to help formulate better lectures

- *English and modern literature*: Emphasise explicit recollection transition and reinforcement from previous lecture. At the start of a session ask students to summarise the main points recently covered. Then make explicit connections between that summary and the new lecture.
- *Chemistry*: Incorporate demonstrations into your lectures. This will lend variety and arouse curiosity in a way that verbal communication alone cannot. For example, colloid solutions can be introduced by combining water and corn starch in certain proportions. What results is a substance that vividly challenges notions of what is a liquid and what is a solid.
- *Computer science and linguistics*: First, present complex ideas in a simplified form, stripped of qualifications and conditions. Once students have this general idea, their minds will be able to more effectively cope with all the demands and details of qualifiers.
- *History*: Students' motivation can be greatly increased if lectures are made more informal and loosely organised, so that discussion is included. This gives students responsibility to raise questions and be involved in their learning. In this type of approach the conclusion of the lecture is very important. It should have a punchy, well-structured conclusion. This will give the students a feeling of a memorable session.
- *Material science and engineering*: Preparation is key here as it is very important to keep students motivated and involved. Ask yourself: What is the fundamental problem or issue that will be approached and tackled? Devise several methods for solving one problem or question. This shows students that problem solving is flexible and has several stages of development.

Summary of points related to lectures

Students will only learn when they are actively engaged in their learning. For the lecture to succeed students need to see not only the relevance of what is being imparted but also the reason for having to learn the information being given. For this to happen they need direction and need to understand individual points and the lecture as a whole. Students need to expend their energy efficiently, and a good, well-structured and co-ordinated lecture is essential for effective student learning to occur. Cohesiveness between parts of the lecture is key. Do not give students endless textbook material. This is both a dry and ineffective way of teaching students, who can obtain that material themselves from references. Add material by making your own information pack for them. This will also motivate students to attend and take part in sessions. Students will remember points much better if they are connected and referenced to other sources of learning.

Using small groups as a teaching strategy

In nearly every text related to teaching and learning in higher education, small group teaching raises the question, 'What is meant by a small group?' (see e.g. Abercrombie, 1970; Bligh, 1986; Ramsden, 1992). The main reason for this discussion is historical in that small group work was seen to be an offshoot of the main teaching method of the lecturer. Advocacy of teaching in small groups cannot be seen as an attack upon the lecture method but as a significant alternative for student learning. This section is concerned with the nature of the teacher–student relationship in small groups, whatever that group is called. The optimum size is between ten and twenty students. Larger classes may also be called seminars, but the types of discussions and activities that might be engaged in by the students will be limited by the size of the group. Abercrombie (1993) suggests that 'the term group means a number of people who are in face-to-face contact, so that each of them can interact with all others' (p. 70). She goes on to say,

> A class cannot be a group if members are too large for each member to be able to interact with each of the others. But nor is a small class necessarily a group, for while a class is in session the teacher may be the only person who interacts with each of all the others, and with whom the others interact.
>
> (p. 70)

Group teaching involves the teacher in deliberately removing him or herself from being the focus of attention. The teacher becomes a facilitator of learning by encouraging students to interact among themselves. If group work is to be successful the size of the group will be a significant factor and depend on its function.

Skill in group teaching needs to be cultivated, in the same way as lecturing or tutoring. These skills may be guided by some general principles about group situations. These include the following:

- *The teacher assumes a different role*: here the teacher must emancipate the students from their dependence on the teacher as the source of knowledge and competence, and to encourage them to be autonomous. What is distinctive here from other forms of higher education teaching is the method by which the teacher encourages autonomy and intellectual growth. It is not dependent on didactic teaching but on encouraging students to interact and learn from each other. This does not mean the teacher takes a back seat; on the contrary, it requires considerable skill to facilitate students to engage in discussion and creative thinking. Stenhouse (1972; p. 98) argues:

> Successful participant small groups in education are likely to be formal rather than informal. They call for rules and conventions. Many seminars fail because tutors see them as informal occasions. . . . The teacher will be most effective if he defines his role and thereby makes his or her use of authority also rule-governed, and his or her area of initiative clear. Small group work is not forwarded by the renunciation of authority, but by its definition. . . . Group rules and teaching roles need to be logically consonant with the demands of an explicit task . . . and need to take account of the psychology of groups. The problem of developing satisfactory small group work depends as much on student training as teacher training.

- *The physical environment in which a group meets*: The importance of face-to-face contact in improving communication cannot be overestimated. Physical proximity is very important in human communication. In face-to-face contact control of intercourse by eye movements is possible (Argyle, 1967). Observing body language and movement by individuals allows the teacher to identify those students feeling awkward or shy or dominating a situation. These human forms of communication can be best detected in a physical environment that is conducive to making the student feel part of the group. If the teacher remains behind a lectern or sits in a position within the room that dictates authority, it is less likely that a good group dynamic will develop. Setting a room up in a horseshoe shape or round table format encourages participation, as no one person – teacher included – dominates the structure in terms of physical presence. Geographical site is also important. The social climate that the group may experience will differ according to where it meets. A class set in a tutor's room or a classroom can affect the interactions within that group.
- *Being aware of student expectations of group work*: The expectations students bring to group work will affect their behaviour, participation and learning outcomes. Many students expect the teacher/tutor to continue in their authoritative role, to which they are accustomed. If students are not explicitly told about the aims and objectives of group work it is possible that hostility and rejection of the method can occur. If you want student learning outcomes to be achieved through group work it is important to construct a plan. To assist in that process consider the following six points

1   How much freedom should you offer students within the group, either for expressing opinions or in the manner in which they express them?

2   How will you maintain a balance between being too controlling and being too permissive?

3   How will you ensure that the time spent in group work will be used constructively?

4   How will you aim to draw all members of the group into the discussion or other activities you have designed for the group to engage in?

5   What techniques will you use to elicit questions from the group, so that there are not too many silent periods?

6   How will you motivate the group and sustain that motivation without talking too much and dominating the group?

Some of the functions of small group work can be categorised into three areas: lecturer–small group interaction; lecturer–student interaction; student–small group interaction.

Lecturer–small group interaction

Within a normal lecture students do not usually have the 'freedom of interruption'; this is one of the perceived weaknesses of the lecture. The lecturer cannot assume a full understanding of all he or she has said and he or she does not know what the students are thinking while the lecture is in progress, unless they are interrupted and questioned. The same argument can be put forward with regard to what extra knowledge the students might wish to know that was not covered during the lecture. If the lecture is within a small group, the teaching strategy and approach to student interaction can be perceived differently. For this to occur the tutor has to be aware of two general points:

1   He or she must provide the opportunity for free discussion with full participation by all members of the group.

2   The development of a special type of relationship between the tutor and his or her students.

To facilitate the development of lecturer–small group interaction both students and tutors have to appreciate that they have equal rights to participate, and any of them may initiate discussion and criticism. This may happen in a number of ways, including the interruption of the lecture or discussion by questioning. Each student is actively encouraged to develop critical thinking, using his or her own judgement and methods of reasoning. Students should also be enabled to learn from each other and not rely on the 'expert' in the form of the tutor/lecturer.

Lecturer–student interaction

This approach applies to areas such as problem solving within a lecture or small group lecture/seminar. The objectives here are to promote the application of new principles and to appreciate some of the problems faced by the group in solving the problem. Here the tutor can 'abdicate' (albeit temporarily) his status as an authority, and take on the role of an interpreter and clarifier of issues being discussed and engaged in within the group. The tutor's superior knowledge and experience allows him or her to ask the right questions to provoke thought or to redirect students in their problem-solving activities. This method allows the tutor to observe the students and to get a feel for what they know or don't know, understand or don't understand, and need to know in the future.

The process of observation and redirected learning of the students allows the tutor to encourage feedback of the students' responses to the problems and possible solutions. The clarification of subject matter, and the discussion of alternative solutions to problems, whether given by other students or by the tutor, are especially valuable aspects of the learning process of small group work where the teaching strategy is based on lecture-student interaction.

Student–small group interaction

The main aim of this type of small group work is to enable students to solve problems and learn by working solely with other students. The principal objective is for students to become proficient in the art of problem solving, decision making, evaluating and applying principles through free discussion, team work and creative application of knowledge. Group practical activities in the sciences, problem solving in mathematics or project work in almost any discipline could be served by student–small group interaction. Simulation exercises are another type of activity that falls within student – small group interaction These may include micro-teaching, computer simulations of medical procedures, examining virtual archaeological sites, or viewing video-tapes of art or drama for critical appraisal. The role of the tutor is to facilitate learning by making sure the group can work together and that the environment in which they have to work is conducive to the tasks set. A significant aspect of this type of group work is that students often express some of their attitudes towards their work and their preferred ways of learning. This can give both the student and the tutor more self-confidence in the way learning tasks are approached (see Table 6.1).

Table 6.1 Summary of small group teaching: a classification

Teaching method	Objectives	Teacher's role	Leader	Time	Size of group	Size of class
Individualised task	• Involvement by all • Problem solving	• Sets of tasks • Poses problems	• None	1–4 min	1	Any
Buzz groups	• Encouraging reticent students • Group cohesion • Consolidate memory by 'rehearsal' of facts • Learn terminology by use • Feedback • Training in discussion techniques	• Set tasks • Ensure formation of groups • Circulate to help groups, meet students, get feedback • Controls reporting back	• None • A 'secretary' may record decisions or answers to problems	2–15 min	2–6 No more than 3 in one row	6 or more
Seminar	• Critical thinking • Ability to present in argument • Thought at all levels	• Usually chooses topic • Preparation of arguments on key issues • Listening	• Teacher	Over 45 min	Same as group	3–14 Only more if teacher is skilled and/or students are mature
Tutorial	• Individual development of student thought, especially at higher levels • Ask questions • Give reasons • Appreciation of other perspectives	• Listening • Encouraging student questions of himself or herself • Sympathy and praise	• Student or none	Indefinite	Same as group	

Points for consideration

Using the above categorisations of small group teaching create a framework for small group teaching based on your discipline. The purpose of the framework is to help speed the planning and preparation of your work with small groups.

The tutorial

A tutorial usually refers to a meeting of an hour or so between a tutor and a few individual students – usually no more than three students – and frequently on a one-to-one basis. The tutorial is a fundamental teaching strategy in higher education because the student, like an apprentice, learns his or her trade by direct contact with a practitioner. Increasingly students coming to university straight from school are used to absorbing information rather than trying to apply and understand that information in a systematic way. Tutorials are a form of teaching that meets the individual needs of students, by helping them understand how their discipline is constructed, the problems associated with the discipline and how they may be investigated. Tutorials personalise the student's learning; they allow the student to develop a relationship with the tutor. This relationship is very important to the development of the student's knowledge base and learning, as the tutor will often be the only academic whom they can directly approach and ask questions. Personal teaching is of great importance to the student's motivation, self-esteem and morale.

Within higher education, reading, writing and discussion are equally important in the development of the autonomous, critical thinking individual as is the attendance of lectures. The basis of nearly all assessments is written work based on the application of knowledge gained from reading, listening and discussion. Writing is the basis of thinking, which requires the student to order his or her thoughts and express them in a way that makes sense to others. The tutorial has a key role to play in this development process for the student. It is the only opportunity for the student to ask individualised questions that can help his or her development in the discipline.

The art of a good tutorial

There are no set rules for conducting tutorials, and as you become more experienced you will find an operational mode that suits both you and your students. However, there are certain issues and rules that you will need to address in the first instance. These include the number of tutorials you will give and what the student entitlement is. Where will you conduct the tutorial, will the tutorial be small group or individual and how will you conduct the tutorial? It is good practice to set tutorial rules for students. Students like to know whether you want to see their work prior to the tutorial, or whether you expect the student to talk through their work and for you to comment or give guidance as the tutorial progresses. These are key points that have to be made explicit to the student.

The extent to which tutors analyse a student's work or comment upon it as a way of eliciting discussion from the student is a personal choice and will develop as the relationship between the student and tutor grows. The main objectives for the tutor should be to ensure that the student:

- Has produced a properly organised account of the subject.
- Understands what he or she has written and that the student has only written what he or she believes to be an accurate support of the argument.
- Leaves with his or her misunderstandings or incorrect perceptions rectified.
- Is encouraged to read further, research the area from a variety of perspectives appropriate to the topic and gain a deep understanding of the issues associated with the problems under investigation.
- Knows the date, time and expectations of the next tutorial.

Points for consideration

Before arranging your tutorials consider the following statements:

- Establishing what you expect from your students during a tutorial.
- Deciding how you want to conduct your tutorials.
- Establishing what you feel the students should gain from the tutorial.
- Establishing ground rules for tutorials so that the students have clear expectations from the tutorial.
- Do you expect students to send you their work prior to the tutorial or will they bring the work with them?

The content of a tutorial

The above task should facilitate how the tutorial will proceed and what the content of the tutorial should be. However, it is equally important to consider the wider implications of tutorial content. A significant question that should be asked is: How is the tutorial related to the lectures the student is studying? Tutorials may be designed to reinforce information given during the lecture, and to extend that information to areas of application such as problem solving or simulations or interpretations of the information given. The responsibility of tutorial content is often delegated to the tutor. It is therefore very important to give serious thought to tutorial content, strategy and achievable learning outcomes from the tutorial process.

Points for consideration

Before arranging your tutorials consider the following questions:

- What is the aim of your tutorial?
- What do you expect your students to learn from your tutorial?
- How will you ensure that the content of your tutorial will achieve the learning outcomes you have set for the tutorial?
- How will you select the content of your tutorial and why have you chosen the content?

The seminar

Seminars for undergraduates should be small enough for realistic discussion in which everyone can find opportunity to take part. Ideally a seminar series should allow all students to present a paper during the series. A seminar is not effective unless there is a common degree of expert knowledge enjoyed by its members. The tutor's role in the seminar is to ensure that a corpus of expert knowledge is available. The seminar offers two elements to teaching and learning. The first relates to the regular meeting of the same group of students working with one another on a group of topics as a continuing syllabus; the second relates to the less frequent meetings that bring students together with senior scholars and researchers for particular occasions. Both types of seminar offer students the opportunity to engage with issues and problems related to their subject area. Each seminar presents different opportunities to students as well. These include the chance to question experts and researchers at the cutting edge of knowledge in their field, and offers the student an opportunity to question fellow students' understanding of similar issues and problems. The role of the tutor is to reflect on the learning outcomes that are desired for the students engaging in the seminar process. From these reflections the tutor should be able to identify, plan and organise seminars that help achieve the stated learning outcomes for the students.

When students participate in seminars they should have a clear understanding of the nature of the learning they are to engage in. These are associated with acquiring skills in communication, thinking and writing rather than the transmission of knowledge.

The seminar should provide the following:

1   Practice in preparing written work for discussion.
2   Practice in discussion.
3   Practice in intelligent and unprejudiced scepticism.
4   Exercise in the use of purposeful discussion to assess new information and theories.
5   Establish student confidence in the art of argument.

Points for consideration

Before arranging a series of seminars for your students, consider the following questions:

- What is the aim of your seminar series or individual seminar?
- What do you expect your students to learn from the seminars?
- How will you ensure that the content of the seminars will achieve the learning outcomes you have set for the tutorial?
- How will you select the content of the seminars and why have you chosen the content?

Teaching with technology

The computer is dramatically changing the way teaching can be perceived, prepared for and delivered. Searching computerised databases, using statistical packages to analyse data, using the Web for information seeking and research and e-mail have become commonplace in the teaching/learning environment. Yet when many new and experienced lecturers step into the lecture room they either ignore technology or rely on technology they are very familiar with, such as the OHP, the blackboard and chalk, textbooks, etc.

For some, the use of IT in teaching and learning is still daunting; however, we cannot ignore the fact that many students are very IT literate and expect technology to be used in teaching and learning. Technology allows teachers to customise their teaching and learning activities to better fit the needs of students. Technology also encourages students to move beyond the lecture theatre to expand their learning and learning-associated activities. A good example here is from English Literature, where students study Shakespeare's plays. Many students have seen some of the plays they have studied. If a CD-Rom with clips of the plays could be accessed, students could interrogate the clips, see the various performances and begin to interpret the plays from a variety of perspectives. Students could be encouraged to conduct such activities as self-directed study, the results of which can be brought to the next lecture or teaching session for discussion and further exploration.

In anthropology 'virtual-field sights' can be used as a means of interrogating extensive data collected from studies both past and present. This allows students to view archaeological sights and artefacts through virtual reality panoramas, thus giving them a significantly enhanced learning environment. Again, students can interrogate the CD-Rom or database as self-directed study and the results may be used in a following session with the lecturer, having the master disk or database live on the day to help discussion and investigation.

In mechanical engineering and science-based disciplines technology can be used to enhance learning through simulations and virtual laboratories, thus allowing students to conduct possibly dangerous experiments without fear or danger to themselves.

The most important aspect of teaching with technology is understanding why you are going to use the technology and to ask the question: Is it the best and most effective way of teaching the topic or problem? The essential principles of using technology for teaching must start with the pedagogical aims and to determine what you are trying to accomplish with your students. There is no point using technology just for the sake of using technology. However, if your aims and learning outcomes can be better achieved through using technology then it is essential it is used, and used effectively, within the teaching session.

As demonstrated in the above examples, technology can bring to reality what verbal communication may often fail to demonstrate. The use of virtual reality in anthropology or history sessions can be invaluable to learning, as are seeing several different performances or clips of the same Shakespeare play for learning about literary interpretation. While technology may be able to facilitate your pedagogical purposes of achieving your aims and learning outcomes, it should not replace your active involvement with the students and the traditional activities that occur in a lecture or teaching session.

Technology is a very effective tool to be used outside of the formal teaching session but inclusive of it. Students should be encouraged to use technologies to enhance and extend their learning through self-directed study. However, the success of such pedagogic practice relies on the teacher following up the activities in teaching sessions and ensuring that students complete the extra tasks.

As with all teaching preparation, technological courseware also needs thought, not only in its form but in the purpose for its use. Technological course material must make students think about and become aware of the learning process they are engaged in. Technological courseware must have the basic teaching principles (discussed in Chapter 2) in mind and especially emphasise the need for students to actively engage with the material and their own learning.

An example here is taken from mathematics, science and technology education (Berkeley UCL). They suggest that thoughtful technological course-ware, like thoughtful teaching, can achieve three important goals. It can:

1   Encourage students to think like experts, including getting them to understand problem-solving processes and to critique solutions to problems.
2   Make thinking visible, so that the process of learning is emphasised, not just the result.
3   Scaffold knowledge, building on what students already know, so that they can understand and form general principles from new information.

In real terms this can mean designing courseware that encourages students to make predictions which can then be tested, whether these are real or virtual experiments. Students can then build their knowledge systematically in their discipline.

Using electronic communication for teaching

Electronic communication allows an immediate response to student queries outside of formal teaching sessions. Such communication can enhance student learning, as students can ask individualised questions and not wait for the next teaching session. When the significance of individualised learning is accepted it presents the lecturer with a very powerful tool for enhancing learning. Due to the asynchronous nature of most electronic tools in use in higher education, students can work at their own pace and level of knowledge. Thus e-mail allows students to ask questions that are of particular relevance to their own learning.

Web-based discussion forums and electronic mailing lists are also significant tools that enhance student participation and individualised learning. Such tools encourage interaction with peers and tutors. Discussions that occur between students have great richness and give a different perspective to the issues or problems being tackled by the formal learning situation.

Online discussion gives shy or quiet students the opportunity to have their say and to participate in discussions they might otherwise have not contributed to.

Taking the plunge and introducing technology into your teaching

If you have decided to include technology in your pedagogic practice it is important that you ascertain what you will expect the students to achieve by using the technology and how best your choice of learning outcomes are to be achieved. Relating the aims and learning outcomes to the learning activity are key aspects for consideration.

When you have identified the learning outcomes to be achieved you can then relate them to the type of learning activity in which the student might engage in order to meet those outcomes. Table 6.2 illustrates the selection process.

Selecting an appropriate technological method

Table 6.3 illustrates the need to consider teaching methods and student learning activities. Many teaching strategies are a synthesis of several methods. The same is true of using technological tools; for example, some technological packages are tutorials, some are simulations and some are role plays or case studies, but each will have a variety of ways in which students will interact with the software.

Points for consideration

The above sections have illustrated the way some of the new technologies can be integrated into teaching and learning. Using your experience of your discipline and courses you have to teach, consider the following questions in conjunction to your practice.

- Could you introduce IT into your teaching?
- Which aspects of IT best fit your discipline and style of teaching?
- How do your course aims and learning outcomes match the technology you have chosen?
- How familiar are you with software packages in your discipline area that can enhance student motivation and participation?

Summary points for consideration

- It is essential to understand that good teaching requires more than the transference of teaching material to a technological format.
- Greater reliance on technology does not necessarily achieve your aims and learning outcomes.
- Technology can be used to improve the quality of instruction.
- Technology can increase motivation of students, as well as encourage quiet and shy individuals to participate in online discussion.
- Technology can offer virtual environments to enhance learning.
- Technology is not cheap, nor is it always reliable; therefore make sure it is within the module budget.

Table 6.2 The selection process

Step	Guideline	Product
1 State aims	What are students expected to achieve in terms of: • knowledge • intellectual skills • practical skills • attitudes	Educational aims
2 Related aims to learning outcomes	How may aims be best achieved: • by students observing • by students listening • by students reading • by students doing	Learning activity appropriate to the aims
3 Selected method	Which teaching/learning method allows for the learning activities appropriate to the aim?	Appropriate method
4 Select medium	Identify media relevant to selected method	Appropriate medium
5 Select equipment or tool and materials	What equipment, tools and materials are appropriate for the learning experience	Appropriate technology

Table 6.3 Examples of teaching methods and technological applicability

Methods	Major student learning activity	Technology
Demonstration and simulation	Observation/manipulation situations	Tools that allow observation followed by virtual application
Lecture/acting	Listening and interpretation	Video clips/CD-ROM, virtual reality
Indirect discourse	Writing, reading critical thinking, question posing	E-mail, online discussion, web-based discussion forums
Research and information gathering	Research skills	Web directories, database
Tutorial	Specific predetermined skill	Tutorial-based exercise
Data interrogation	Application of data	Statistical packages, data interpreters

Discussion as a way of teaching and learning

Brookfield (1991) suggests that there are fifteen benefits to using discussion as a teaching strategy in higher education. Some of these points include:

- Helping students explore a diversity of perspectives.
- Increasing students' awareness of and tolerance for ambiguity or complexity.
- Helping students recognise and investigate their assumptions.
- Increasing intellectual agility.
- Helping students develop collaborative habits.
- Helping students develop skills of synthesis and integration.

(p. 17)

'Discussion is one of the most effective ways to make students aware of the range of interpretations that are possible in an area of intellectual inquiry' (ibid., p. 18). Essentially, discussion is a key element of student learning. Discussion promotes active participation and helps to develop tolerance and collaborative forms of working. However, discussion is not always easy to instigate, or, once instigated, to keep under control. So how can lecturers increase the quantity and ensure the quality of discussion as a means of student learning?

Framing discussion sessions

As a discussion leader the lecturer is dependent on the group: its level of preparation, its enthusiasm, and its willingness to participate. Good planning is essential to any discussion group. Like the preparation of any teaching and learning session it is important to establish your aims and objectives/learning outcomes for your discussion session. You should consider the following questions when planning for discussion:

- Do you want the students to apply newly learned skills?
- Do you want the students to mull over new subject matter?
- Do you want the students to learn to analyse arguments critically?
- Do you want the students to see problems?
- Do you want the students to become motivated to do research?

These questions are not mutually exclusive, but they require different types of leadership on the part of the tutor or lecturer and different responses on the part of the students. You may wish to be directive throughout the discussion or you may wish to be non-directive and allow the students to determine the flow of the discussion. Which ever route is chosen, you will have to think about the nature of the questions you will ask to get the discussion started.

Asking questions

Prior to a discussion session it may be worth considering the nature of the material you will give students to ensure that the discussion covers the areas or topic you wish the students to learn about. Distributing study questions prior to the session demonstrates not only your own interest but helps the students to focus their preparations for the discussion sessions.

The types of questions you use to start a discussion session vary in effectiveness and can considerably influence the success of the session. For this reason it is important to spend some time preparing the types of questions you think you should use. It is useful to think of these in order of difficulty or complexity. Start with easily answered questions to build confidence, then progress to more challenging and finally more complex questions. A pattern you may wish to consider is exemplified below:

- Make your starting point work with which the student is familiar or feels comfortable with. This might be a series of questions based on common sense or from basic information gained from the subject area.
- Use questions that encourage students to explain relationships between the units of information they have been given with a view to forming general concepts.
- Use questions that encourage students to apply concepts and principles they have learned to new data and different situations.

Increasing the difficulty and complexity of questions requires planning and a deep understanding of the discipline area you are trying to promote. Below is an example taken from a discussion session in philosophy, based on Plato's *Republic*. The questioning fell into three sections of difficulty. The first related to questions of understanding, the second to exploring relationships between concepts, and the third to application of knowledge.

Section 1

You might begin by asking questions such as:

- What are the basic components of Plato's ideal state?
- What are the characteristics of a good ruler?
- Why does Plato ban poetry from his republic?

Section 2

Having established that the students understand the material, questions should become more probing and aim at the students drawing connections and making relationships between the concepts; for example:

- How does the allegory of the cave fit into the rest of the work?
- What criticisms of Athenian society is Plato making?

Section 3

This involves asking students questions that make them apply their knowledge; for example:

- Is Plato's republic a desirable place to live?
- How would Plato criticise a contemporary British university?

The art of structuring questions is only half the battle in engaging students in discussion. The way you ask the questions and who you ask them to are equally important, and will influence the effectiveness of the discussion and ultimately the students' learning. Group dynamics are very important to making discussion sessions operational.

Points for consideration

You may wish to consider the following points prior to your discussion session:

- Decide whether to ask questions of specific individuals in the group or the whole group.
- Consider how much time you would like to leave between questions.
- Consider how long to leave a silence before answering the question yourself.
- Structure your questions so that they do not invite a programmed response.

Increasing participation

A successful discussion leader is one who formulates good questions and considers how best to use these questions in a discussion session. However, despite good planning and preparation, there still remains the task of making sure that participation by all students occurs. For this to happen the following points may help shape the structuring of your session:

1   Encourage participation by all students in the group.
2   Keep the conversation flowing by encouraging the students to talk to each other, not just to you.

3 Try to help the students in their articulation of complex issues by giving insight into the material under discussion.
4 Think of interventions that encourage further investigation into the topic. These may be questions such as:

- Can you put that another way?
- Can you give an example of your description?
- What do you mean by that?

Or body language such as:

- Circular hand movements that indicate more is required.
- Smiling showing approval and encouragement.
- Showing active listening on your behalf rather than continual interjection.

These elements are suggestions to increase participation. The one key element to remember is: *Do not dominate the discussion.*

Sustaining discussion

Once a discussion has taken off and is focused, students will start discussions amongst themselves. Here you have to become a moderator, mediator and a summariser of information. Creating a good climate for a discussion group is essential. This will be greatly assisted if you are as relaxed and unselfconscious as possible. Enjoy the situation and watch your students flourish through guided discussion. Students enjoy the spontaneity and excitement of learning through discussion. Student opinions have to be respected and shown respect (even if you think they are outlandish). After all, discussion is a joint learning exercise. Students learn from each other as well as the lecturer, but the lecturer also learns from his or her students.

Summary of discussion as a way of teaching and learning

The main point to remember when planning teaching and learning sessions that involve discussion is *'Facilitate, don't dominate'*.

Prepare well

- Consider your objectives/learning outcomes for the discussion. What do you hope to accomplish?
- What topics or subject areas would you like discussed and which areas would you consider being tangential?
- Ensure your students have enough previous knowledge so that a constructive discussion can take place.

- Use discussion sessions to help students make connections and relationships with concepts and material they have engaged with.
- Develop your questions in such a way that they will facilitate discussion and prompt critical thinking.

Facilitate discussion

- Develop and provide guidelines for participation in discussion sessions. Discuss these with students, stick to them and enforce them during the session.
- Use open-ended questions, asking students for clarification and examples as a way of maintaining discussion.
- Encourage students to talk to one another.
- Give students time to reflect and pause for thought.
- Control the 'talkers' and 'non-talkers'.
- Towards the end of the session sum up the main points so that the students have a clear picture of what has been discussed and learned from the session.

Evaluate the discussion session

- Notice how many students participated in the discussion.
- Make a note of who contributed and who did not. Things to look for include gender, ethnicity, shyness or reluctance to talk.
- How did the students react to the content of the discussion?
- Did students respect each other's views and was the discussion orderly?
- How far off the subject did the discussion go, if at all?
- Ask students to evaluate the session and determine what they think they have learned from the discussion.
- Compare student views of learning with your stated learning outcomes.

Points for consideration

Using the above summary, plan a discussion session based on learning outcomes. Devise a series of questions and prompts that you feel will stimulate discussion and encourage students to critically engage with the subject matter of that discussion.

Final comments

Developing successful teaching strategies takes time, good planning and a clear understanding of aims and learning outcomes. Success in the classroom, lecture theatre or laboratory also relies on choosing the most appropriate teaching strategy for the occasion. This chapter has concentrated on some of the main teaching and learning approaches found in higher education. They are not mutually exclusive, nor are they the only methods. However, what this chapter has attempted to do is introduce the basic elements of each approach, bringing to the forefront aspects that can be developed, worked on and evaluated in such a way as to prompt further practice in teaching strategies.

Chapter 7

Assessment

Introduction

Assessment, recording and reporting are key issues that relate to all areas of teaching, learning and development within higher education. Assessment has several forms and is needed for a variety of purposes within teaching and learning. It provides information on individual student progress, helps academic tutors to address areas of weakness, and gives both tutor and student information about their academic progress. Assessing students' work is not a new venture, but within the past five years greater emphasis has been placed on alternative ways of assessing students in higher education, both formally through standardised university examinations and informally through tutor assessment.

This chapter will be divided into two areas: that of assessment, and that of recording and reporting. This will help focus on the specific issues and problems within each topic. The chapter will first discuss the relevant issues related to assessment, recording and reporting. This will involve looking at what assessment is, the form it takes, and the relevance it has to teaching and learning. At the end of each section points for consideration will be given to help the process of understanding assessment within the context of the learning environment.

Promoting student learning is a principal aim of higher education. Assessment lies at the heart of this process. It can provide a framework in which educational learning outcomes/objectives may be set, and students' progress recorded and reported. It can yield a basis for planning the next educational steps in response to students' needs, and by facilitating dialogue between tutors and students it can enhance professional skills and help the faculty as a whole to strengthen learning across a variety of programmes, courses and modules. This suggests that assessment of students' learning and progress is central to effective teaching and learning. Reactions to assessment are rarely neutral; they are frequently influenced by prior experience and exposure to the assessment process, either as students in school, students in higher education or professional activities.

In recent years the academics' role in assessment has become a central task, with increased numbers of students taking a greater number and variety of modules, thus creating an increased workload. A consequence of this increased load has been the need for academics to gain greater organisational skills so that assessment tasks can be conducted systematically and effectively.

Purpose of assessment

All forms of assessment provide estimates of the individual's current status and should primarily be concerned with providing guidance and feedback to the learner. The position taken here is that feedback that creates a learning environment is the central and most important function of assessment in relation to student learning. The results of assessment may be used for judgemental and for developmental purposes. Figure 7.1 shows how assessment may be characterised to show the continuum from judgemental to developmental. In this context developmental assessment is concerned with improving the students' learning; this is directly related to and founded on trust between individuals and their tutors. Judgemental assessment is concerned with licence to proceed and allied to accountability and accreditation.

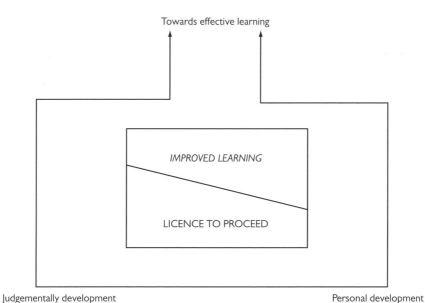

Figure 7.1 Assessment and development

Establishing reasons why students need to be assessed requires an understanding of the purposes of assessment. The general purposes in relation to teaching and learning and student development may be summarised in the following ways:

- Provide feedback to improve learning.
- Motivate individuals.
- Diagnose strengths and weaknesses.
- Help develop skills of self-assessment.
- Provide a profile of what has been learned or developed.
- Pass or fail individuals.
- Licence to proceed.
- Licence to practice.
- Predict success in future employment.

The above list can be divided into two main purposes; one relates to feedback and the other relates to accreditation and accountability. The first is intended to improve the quality of teaching and learning through reflection and reflective practice. Students engage in the problems and discourses of their disciplines and are given encouragement, response and feedback on what they do, as appropriate, with a view to the becoming more independent, critical and reflective thinkers. This is developmental or formative assessment, a type of assessment that allows the student to learn from their assessed performance.

For the new and experienced academic it is essential to understand the range and purposes that surround assessment, and to distinguish between the different procedures, namely formative, summative and diagnostic assessment.

Formative assessment

Formative assessment is an ongoing process that tutors are involved in at two levels, formal and informal. It reflects the way tutors absorb the information and evidence related to student learning, and how they use it to inform their future teaching sessions, whether this is the next task or series of tasks. The nature of this form of assessment is to promote effective further learning by students. It may be achieved in a variety of ways, including:

- Giving students helpful feedback.
- Giving the tutor feedback.
- Identifying students' future learning needs.

The main focus of formative assessment is to identify errors, difficulties and shortcomings in students' work. It also informs the tutor of the nature of advice and information needed to be given to the students so that they can improve their future learning outcomes.

Without formative assessment tutors could not function effectively. However, formative assessment is less useful for those who wish to have definite information about students' progress. The main audience here is students and their peers, colleagues within the faculty, and potential employers. This type of audience requires a summary of achievement and progress in order to give an accurate picture of the students' learning. This is referred to as *summative assessment.*

Summative assessment

Summative assessment is directly related to accreditation of knowledge or performance. Here the student is certified for his or her achievements. At present this occurs primarily through a variety of examinations. Summative assessment takes into account a variety of components such as written assessments, project work, observation, and tutor evaluations. In such cases judgements are made and judgemental assessment or summative assessment occurs, thus producing a decision for the record. Such a decision would reflect whether or not the individual has reached the required standard. Summative assessment identifies the standard of attainment achieved by an individual at a given moment in time, normally carried out at the end of a period of teaching or instruction. This would include end-of-module exams, and end-of-course/programme assessments. The outcomes of such assessments are typically grades, or percentages used by schools, faculty or departments to determine level of attainment, degree of classification or conferment of a thesis.

Formative and summative assessment can and often do get confused in practice. The essence of formative assessment is that it provides feedback to the academic during the learning and developmental period, and it should provide the type of information that gives the academic the opportunity to improve and learn from that feedback.

In both formative and summative assessment judgements are made, the difference being, in the first, that it directly serves the needs of the academic and student. In the second, it primarily serves the needs of the external community, employers or institutions for study.

The role of assessment

The above description establishes the purposes of assessment; equally important is the role of assessment and how that fits within a development framework of a student. The central argument put forward here is that assessment has two definitive roles: that of accountability from an institutional perspective and one from the individuals perspective, and that of development and enhanced learning opportunities.

Before assessing any phenomenon it is necessary to know what that phenomenon is. In Chapter 3, a description has been given as to the nature of learning that students may be engaged in. These approaches can, and should, impact on the nature of assessment for the individual concerned. Thus the central premise is that any assessment that is conducted should assist the student to learn and provide feedback that encourages reflection both on a personal and academic level. In Chapter 3, learning is defined essentially as changes in knowledge, understanding, skills and attitudes brought about by experience and reflection upon that experience, whether or not that experience is structured. If learning of this nature is to occur, assessment must be used in a way that will enhance the above definition of learning.

Assessment of students must reflect the specific processes of learning they have been engaged in. However, at present many academics assess through traditional assessment strategies, often ignoring the fact that teaching may take a process-orientated route. A consequence of this is that academics include assessment strategies that tend to examine what students have memorised rather than whether they can apply, analyse and critically reflect on what they have learned. Thus assessment needs to be an integral part of the development process that focuses on student learning.

Some reasons for assessing

The term 'assessment' is used in this chapter for any type of activity which is employed to determine how successfully students have achieved course aims and learning outcomes.

Assessment may also be held for other purposes, some of which are listed below:

- To illustrate the meaning of learning outcomes and aims.
- To provide feedback to students.
- To provide feedback to academics.
- To compare one student's score with scores obtained by other students; this is often part of a selection process.
- To compare one student's score in a test with his or her score in a different test.
- To compare a student's score with a set of norms.
- To compare a student's score with other aspects of assessment.

Some of these reasons have been discussed in relation to formative and summative assessment. However, as tutors it is essential that we know how well or how badly our students are learning. This requires being able to compare student against student, and student against a whole group, class or year. Each type of comparison requires an understanding of what and how assessment results may be compared in a valid and reliable way.

Assessment is a measurement, and as such requires instruments and tools that reflect the nature and context of the learning that is being assessed. Hence the measuring instrument(s) employed and the frequency of application will be partially determined by the reason(s) why assessment is being undertaken. Assessment (whether it is in a multiple-choice format, open-ended, open-book essay type, practical or observational) is only one kind of assessment procedure. Assessment should be closely linked to the rest of the programme development processes; such a model has been put forward and discussed in Chapter 5. It is therefore important to consider which type of assessment technique is chosen, as this should depend on the aims and learning outcomes that are selected for the programme, course, module or individual learning session. For example, objective questions are useful for assessing some aims; essays are better for others; and direct assessment using agreed norms is the most appropriate technique for others. It is difficult to assess effectively unless both staff and students know the aims of a course. A long list of all aims and specific learning outcomes is not necessary: a short classification is sufficient for assessment purposes. The importance of this essential (first) step cannot be over-emphasised. Equally, it must be recognised that no one type of assessment can assess all course aims and learning outcomes effectively, and accepting this is key to successful assessment of any given programme.

Appreciating the limitations of assessment procedures will help in establishing student learning outcomes. A number of common failings with assessment procedures are highlighted below:

- Too heavy a reliance on subjective judgement.
- Reliance on absolute standards of judgement.
- Hasty assessment preparation.
- Use of short, inefficient assessment tools.
- Testing trivia.
- Careless wording of assessment questions.
- Neglect of sampling errors.
- Failure to analyse the quality of the test.

One of the purposes of this section is to help prevent the above from occurring.

To assist in the underlying principles of assessment there are a number of key terms that need to be considered, and their functions recognised and understood within an assessment framework.

Key terms of assessment

Norm-referenced assessment

In norm-referenced assessment all the students' scores are put into a graph and a certain percentage assigned to each grade (e.g. only 10 per cent will gain a first, 20 per cent a 2.1 and so on). Alternatively a cut-off point is chosen for passing, allowing a certain percentage to pass and the rest to fail. What this reflects is that the classification a student achieves and whether they pass or fail partly depends on the performance of the other students.

Criterion-referenced assessment

These types of assessment tasks are designed to reflect whether or not a student can do a specific task, or range of tasks, as opposed to measuring how good or how bad a student's performance is in relation to other students.

In criterion-referenced assessments, levels of achievement or criteria of performance are set and students are marked or graded according to whether they reach the level of attainment. In this form of assessment there is no limit to how many students achieve a given level.

Forms of assessment

Internal assessment

These are tutor-orientated tasks. They are devised, implemented and marked by the module tutor. The tutor, as part of his or her own teaching programme often uses internal assessment. These can be tests, projects or practical tasks. Internal assessment informs the tutor of continual individual progress.

External assessment

External assessment can often take place when students are on industrial placement. Such activities and tasks are devised by the placement and are moderated in conjunction with the higher education institution.

Informal/formal assessment

This type of assessment takes place as part of normal classroom life and practice. It is usually observational, where the tutor observes performance and makes notes for future reference. Formal assessment is made following prior warning that assessment will occur. This gives students the opportunity to revise and prepare for the assessment activities.

Continuous/terminal assessment

Increasingly, continuous assessment is becoming a significant method by which students are assessed. It requires tutors/assessors to base the final assessment on the standard of attainment achieved on a variety of pieces of work over a long period of time. This technique is particularly relevant to final qualifications. Terminal assessment is based on standards of achievement reached at the end of a course, module or programme of work.

Before deciding to embark on 'continual' assessment, the following questions should be considered:

1   Is the assessment of progress throughout the year being sought, or is it sufficient to know a student's achievement at the end of the year?
2   Is it fair to allocate marks to an assessment that takes place early on in the course?
3   Is this the best way to assess particular aims?
4   Is the form of 'continuous' assessment that is being considered compatible with university education?
5   Is it possible to ensure that the work presented is the student's own?
6   Would the strain imposed on students (and staff) on the introduction of continuous assessment be too great?

It is possible that some aims (e.g. those achieved in practical work or in writing essays) are best assessed on a number of occasions outside a formal examination room. Increasing a number of assessments will increase reliability. However, caution is needed in the number of staff involved in marking essays throughout the year, as this can produce complications too.

Each type of assessment has to be chosen and used in the context of teaching and learning environments. It is important to appreciate and understand the rationale of each type of assessment so that appropriate assessment can be chosen to match the purpose.

Using assessment effectively

As stated above, assessment has many faces and can be used for a variety of purposes; however, there are three fundamental reasons for assessment.

1 Feedback

Feedback gives information about students' progress, which in turn allows the tutor to evaluate how effective their teaching has been in achieving the learning outcomes set out within the module, course or programme. Establishing how well learning outcomes have been achieved allows the tutor to correct misunderstandings, give remedial help if required, or stretch students who have been finding the work too easy. Assessment also gives direct feedback to students. It shows them where their performance is in relation to other students, as well as national standards or expected standards. Feedback can direct students in their own improvement.

2 Progress

Assessment is a vital tool for recording and monitoring student progress over the short and long term. These records should help inform tutors of any decisions they need to make about helping future learning needs of students. Records of progress are key lines of communication for tutors, students and fellow colleagues. Records of progress should be key to tutors' long-term planning.

3 Motivation

This is a key factor in encouraging students to achieve what is expected of them. It makes students organise and learn the required work. Motivation can be intrinsic and extrinsic, and in many instances both. Positive feedback and success in assessment tasks is a very effective mechanism for future improvement and motivation.

Points for consideration

- Within your discipline, consider and establish the types of assessment that take place within your faculty and evaluate the purposes for which they are used.
- Try to investigate and understand how these assessment activities help student learning outcomes.
- Establish what forms of assessment are used and whether there is a balance between formative and summative assessment.

Assessing in the learning environment

This can take many forms, but in the first instance a new academic will be involved in the following aspects:

- marking;
- everyday learning tasks;
- project work;
- setting form standardised examinations;
- creating tutor based assessments.

Each form of assessment is important, but a clear perspective must be kept of the purpose or purposes of the chosen assessment. With practice and experience, as new academics develop their teaching skills, so will their assessment techniques develop. The main road to success is to set achievable targets for learning the skills and techniques of assessment. Clear collective goals derived from experience, and practice and discussions with senior colleagues will be a most productive route. Tutor assessment has a significant impact on students' daily lives as well as the tutor's own practice.

Marking

The informal in-session, everyday assessment of students' work is as important as standardised assessment. What are tutors trying to do when they mark students' work and what are the essential elements of marking?

1   Marking takes up a great deal of tutor time; it is therefore important to understand its significance in terms of assessing in the learning environment.
2   Marking work during and after sessions needs to be thorough, systematic, constructive, and returned to students in good time.
3   Marking should give students informative feedback and satisfaction.
4   Good marking motivates students to achieve more.

It is important to realise that marking students' work can have a profound effect on the way students perceive themselves and their self-esteem. Even a simple formative comment can influence a student's future performance. Students like having targets and goals to aim for and respond to; they also acknowledge praise and constructive criticism. All marking routines should aim to encapsulate the above points.

Points for consideration

There should be an assessment policy within your faculty. Examine how your views and knowledge of marking fit in with the established policy.

What can marking be used for?

Marking has two distinct stakeholders, the students and the tutor. Both should use marking as a means of raising achievement and attainment.

From the tutor's perspective marking should:

- Check student understanding.
- Direct future lesson planning and teaching.
- Monitor progress through collection of marks.
- Help assess student progress and attainment.
- Set work of appropriate levels.
- Have clear objectives about what and how you teach.
- Inform students and parents formatively, and summatively.

From the students' perspective marking should and could help them:

- Identify carelessness.
- Proof-reading – i.e. by making them check their work for spelling, punctuation etc.
- Draft work – students can become actively involved in improving their own work.
- Identify areas of weakness and strength.
- Identify areas that lack understanding and knowledge.
- Become more motivated and value their work.

Marking should make the tutor focus on specific issues. The above has identified two perspectives: that of the student and that of the tutor. Both elements need to work in harmony to create a positive environment for students' learning. Marking provides the tutor with many vehicles for learning. Marking procedures involve a variety of skills, and it is essential to understand and identify which skills are being using when marking students' work. For example, marking can be used for:

- Establishing levels of understanding within the whole student cohort.
- Identifying competence within the subject base.
- Identifying areas of work that need revisiting and reinforcing.

- Testing factual knowledge.
- Accuracy in completing and recording experimental or practical work.

Each of these examples focuses on outcomes, and marking should also make the tutor focus on purpose. This means the purpose for which tutors set the work that is to be marked. Fitness for purpose is essential to good marking, recording and eventually reporting.

Points for consideration

Within your course or module what are the aims of the work being set and assessed?

- Checking that the work has been completed.
- Establishing levels of understanding.
- Judging progress in relation to topic and concepts within topic area.
- Making an overall assessment of students' attainment over a long period of time.

The answers to the above should guide what is marked, how the work is set and what use is made of the assessment outcomes.

Marking is an activity that is public; this means that all those who have access to students' work can see what has been marked or ignored. This open scrutiny by students, colleagues, senior tutors and QAA can give a quick judgement about the tutor's approach. It is always good practice to be consistent, systematic and constructive in the marking of students' work.

Assessment and marking check-list

Do the exam problems or questions that the students have been set offer a reasonable expectation of being tackled and that the students can prepare for? Do the questions or problems reflect your aims and learning outcomes of the course or module?

- Make old exam papers available for revision if possible.
- Make clear before any assessment what material you consider important.
- Compare material in the assessment to your major topics and tasks covered in the module to make sure you have been consistent.

Is the assessment a reasonable and accomplishable length?

- Take the assessment yourself. You should be able to finish it in a quarter of the time allocated to the students.

Are the directions and format of the assessment clear and well organised? Is it clear how much each question is worth?

- Ask a colleague to read over the assessment instructions as a way of spotting ambiguities or misleading statements.
- Make sure the print is clear and that, if there is a space left for problems it is of a suitable length.
- Make sure that the value of each question is clear.

Does the assessment start with problems that undermine student confidence? Always start with a problem that will enable students to perform.

Since the level to which students study is influenced by the type of assessment they anticipate, will this assessment signal the need for deep, rigorous teaching?

Marking and grading

- Think out your assessment policy beforehand, write it into the course module and student handbook and stick to it.
- When marking student assessments try not to know whose work you are marking. If you do recognise the handwriting, try to be aware of bias.
- Look over between five and ten assessments before you actually start marking and grading to see how the assessment went and to sort out your standards.
- If possible, grade question by question, not assessment by assessment, as this helps promote consistency.
- Maintain complete marking and grading records of the results of each assessment, so that you can spot problems in any of your assessments.
- Keep old assessment papers to hand out to students in the future, as reviews before assessment or as student self-directed study.

Using everyday learning environments for assessment

Assessment is both essential and integral to effective teaching and student learning. As discussed above, there are many different ways to assess students' work. The everyday learning environment is an excellent way of collecting a variety of information about students. Conventional marking is just one form of assessment. Observation, questioning and listening are also key components of the skills of assessment, all of which need to be practised and developed.

Evidence of students' work can be collected from:

- oral work, such as reading, discussion, questions, role play;
- written work, investigations, experiment notes;
- design work, models, drawings, construction;
- physical skills, co-ordination and manipulative skills.

A broad outlook of students' potential allows the tutor to gain evidence of progress from a wide variety of activities, and as a result to report the extent of student achievement. Monitoring work that is engaged in any learning environment will produce evidence of learning. Both formal and informal session assessments are important, as they allow the tutor to make judgements about student progress and alter their style of teaching to facilitate learning. Feedback from students enables tutors to measure effectiveness of a lesson.

As a tutor there is a need to distinguish between monitoring informally through integrating assessment tasks into normal activities and setting formalised tests. For example, a tutor observing a student conduct an experiment can be used as a means of encouraging and estimating progress or can be used as a means of predicting the student's level of practical knowledge. Similarly the tutor might well question the student to assess his or her level of understanding so that individualised help can be given in a positive way. In each case the student needs to know what the tutor is doing and why. The purpose of the assessment and monitoring has to be clear to tutor and student alike. Skilful assessment of students' progress in meeting the aims and learning outcomes of a course or programme depends very much on how well assessment tasks are integrated into the course so that there is progression in learning.

Tutor-based assessment

It has been stated earlier in this chapter that tutors are assessing students in a variety of ways all the time. But what is tutor-based assessment, and how is it functional in the learning environment? Tutor-based assessment may include:

1   *Written assessments.* These can motivate students to study and learn in preparation for a formal test.
2   *Observation-based assessments.* These look at student performance, whether practical skills such as art, drama, experimentation, etc. can all be assessed by the tutor.
3   *Communication-based assessments.* Students presenting findings, speaking a foreign language, discussing and debating pre-researched work.

All assessment activities need to have purpose, clarity and a clear focus. There are several points that need to be considered prior to planning any assessment activity:

- Tutor-based assessment over a long period of time should be varied to cover a wide range of learning outcomes.
- The assessment task should actually assess that which was intended to be assessed.
- Assessment should relate to intended learning outcomes appropriate to the course or programme requirements.
- All assessment tasks should be fair by way of assessing work covered, enabling students to have the opportunity to perform well.

It is important to realise that the nature of the student's assessment activity will determine the tutor's action in actually marking the assessment. If the student is expected to read aloud, the tutor is expected to listen. If a student performs a practical task the tutor is expected to observe. Hence the tutor's role in this type of assessment activity is crucial. The responsibility of assessing lies with the tutor, irrespective of whether it is just a session or an entire course that is being assessed.

Essentials of tutor-based assessment

- Do not over-assess – quantity of assessment is no substitute for quality teaching and quality assessment.
- Plan work or topic areas thoroughly so that assessment becomes an integral part of the planning routine rather than an add-on activity.
- Spend time developing assessment strategies and techniques. Don't rush the design of a test; a bad test shows nothing while a good test helps tutor and student.
- Incorporate course or programme requirements into the planning of assessment criteria.
- Get a second opinion, show colleagues the assessment procedures intended to be used. A more distanced view can help focus on what the tutor *actually* wants to assess, not what they *think* they are assessing.

Assessment tools

The main types of assessment that are used in higher education include:

Objective assessment

(a) Alternative responses
(b) Multiple choice

(c) Matching:

- Essay
- Short answer
- Structured
- Open book
- Précis
- Project work
- Comprehension
- Practical
- Direct assessment
- Student self-assessment (and peer assessment)
- Oral
- Observation
- Presentation.

A brief description and a summary of the advantages and disadvantages of each type is given below in note form to enable quick reference. A more complete coverage may be found in any text related to assessment. Brown (1997) is to be recommended.

(a) Alternative response

Students are asked to select one of two responses, e.g. true/false or yes/no.

ADVANTAGES

- Large areas of the syllabus can be covered.
- They are easy to write.
- Someone can rapidly mark them without knowledge of the subject or by computer and optical scanning.

DISADVANTAGES

- Ambiguity easily arises.
- Most statements demanding true/false answers are fairly trivial.
- Guessing is encouraged, but can be corrected.

PRECAUTIONS

- Try to select statements that are short, simple and contain only one idea.
- Do not insert the word 'not' in a true statement.
- Make sure 'true' answers are randomly arranged.
- Avoid words such as 'sometimes' or 'usually' in true statements, and 'always' or 'impossible' in false statements.

(b) Multiple choice

Multiple-choice assessment is an attractive alternative for those looking for a faster way of assessing student learning, but there are drawbacks. Multiple-choice papers need time invested in their construction and preparation, plus the questions have to be both challenging and assessing of deep learning and higher cognitive thinking. Multiple-choice assessment is useful for summative purposes, and can give clear directions for future planning and teaching. To design a multiple-choice paper requires a framework for development and an understanding of the terminology associated with such assessment.

The terminology associated with multiple choice is illustrated in Table 7.1, which is followed by Table 7.2, a framework for constructing a multiple-choice assessment.

Table 7.1 Terminology for multiple-choice assessment

Stem	Initial statement or question, called the 'item'
Options	The alternatives
Key	Correct response
Distracters	Options other than correct answer
Faculty index	Number of students giving correct response to an item
Favoured wrong response	The most common wrong response by a group of students
Discrimination	Measure of difficulty of the item

Table 7.2 Framework for constructing a multiple-choice assessment

1	Keep a directory of items
2	Collect items from other members of staff
3	Challenging questions require you to think of the problem first, then translate into multiple-choice questions – and check
4	Avoid using 'not' and 'always' in the stem
5	Use plausible distracters
6	Ask other members of staff to evaluate draft assessment
7	Revise following feedback
8	Try them out on staff or different group of students

Points for consideration

Having designed a draft multiple-choice paper, consider the following questions:

1   What does the paper test?
2   Have all the responses in each stem got some form of plausibility?
3   Is the wording of the paper precise enough?

4   Are all the responses to each stem about the same length?
5   Is the lettering and numbering consistent throughout the paper?
6   How are the results of the assessment going to be utilised?
7   How closely do the items relate to the learning outcomes of the programme/course/module?

Advantages and disadvantages of using multiple-choice assessment

The advantages and disadvantages of using multiple-choice assessment are listed below.

ADVANTAGES

- Large areas of the syllabus can be covered.
- Many cognitive abilities can be tested.
- Someone can rapidly mark them without knowledge of the subject, or by machine.
- Careful analysis of the test results is possible.
- Individual item difficulties and discriminations can be calculated.
- High reliability is possible.
- Speedy reporting of assessment results is possible.

DISADVANTAGES

- Good items are difficult to write and not everyone is capable of writing them.
- A lot of time is required to construct a test.
- Guessing is encouraged, but can be corrected.

PRECAUTIONS

- Avoid ambiguities.
- All responses should be of similar length.
- Responses should be equally plausible to the uninformed.
- Do not include two responses which are opposite in meaning.
- The stem is best presented as a question.
- If the stem is an incomplete statement, ensure that all responses follow from the stem.
- The correct responses should be randomly distributed in the test.
- If the word 'not' is included in the stem, ensure that it is emphasised. In general, however, do not include the word 'not' in the stem.
- If complex data are included in the stem, try to devise a series of multiple-choice questions using the same data.

- Unless you have a good reason, do not make your last response 'none of the above'.
- Make responses as short as possible.
- List responses; do not write them as a complete paragraph.

(c) Matching

Matching questions consists of the questions and instructions, and two lists (called the 'premises' and the 'responses'). The assessment (or questions) instructions explain how matching is to be recorded.

ADVANTAGES

- Large areas of the syllabus can be assessed.
- Someone can rapidly mark them without knowledge of the subject, or by machine.

DISADVANTAGES

- Higher order cognitive abilities are difficult to test.

PRECAUTIONS

- It is best if the list of responses is kept reasonably short, otherwise it can take a long time to answer one question.
- It is essential that the instructions explaining how matching is to be recorded should be absolutely clear.
- The premise and response lists should be arranged in logical order (e.g. numbers should be listed from the highest to the lowest).

(d) Essays

Essays can be a valuable way to assess active learning. In essay questions, the student is allowed to select and organise material in the way which seems to be important to him or her, and no single answer may be said to be 'right' or 'wrong'. However, attached to essay-based assessment are the problems associated with marking. Often a choice of questions is offered in essay questions, and this can lead to a low-test reliability. Also, statistical corrections to marks cannot be done. (When a choice is offered, students are actually answering a number of different examination papers, not merely a single one.) A good text to refer to for further reading is Hounsell (1985).

As a variety of assessment tools are used within one programme, course or module, it is important to be able to compare each method.

Multiple-choice assessment is often compared with essay questions. The following lists some of the pros and cons of both types of assessment.

Multiple choice	*Essay*
Permits guessing	Permits bluffing
Much time devoted to setting	Much time devoted to marking
Machine marked	Subject specialist marked
Student not allowed to express him or herself	Student encouraged to express his or herself
Good for factual knowledge	Poor for factual knowledge
Can test high cognitive skills	Can test high cognitive skills
Large field of knowledge covered by many questions	Small field of knowledge covered by a few questions
Answers generally only right or wrong	Marker can comment on student's reasoning

There have been and continue to be many arguments regarding the benefits or shortfalls of these two forms of assessment. The basis of these disagreements is that multiple choice favours the superficially brilliant over the creatively profound. Some research suggests that multiple-choice questions are concerned with 'convergent' thinking and that essays should be used to test 'creative' thinking. What this points to is that the academic must know what type of knowledge or thinking they are hoping to assess. If recall, understanding of facts and principles and some forms of problem solving are to be tested, then multiple-choice questions are worth considering.

Recording and reporting

Record keeping is a key feature of teaching and assessment. However, if this activity is to be completed efficiently and effectively two questions have to be addressed. Why do tutors keep records of students' work, who are they for, and what is their value?

A prime purpose for record keeping is to help monitor the progress of individual students and plan their future learning. QAA continually state the importance and need for tutors to keep good records of student progress. One of the many reasons for this is that it shows that tutors have fulfilled their responsibilities such as meeting the aims and learning outcomes of the programme, as well as monitoring students' progress throughout the programme of study.

There are three main reasons for record keeping:

1   To monitor and plan ahead.
2   To inform others.
3   To demonstrate that these purposes are being properly followed.

Points for consideration

- What is your faculty/school/department's policy on recording and reporting student progress?
- How have you built recording and reporting progress into your teaching strategies?

Keeping good records

Thinking about good and effective record keeping requires an understanding of the usefulness of records. There are two areas that need to be addressed: (1) the detail/quantity of information to be recorded, and (2) how the information is going to be used. After all, records that are too detailed, dense and incomprehensible have very little chance of being used. Three main functions of good record keeping need to be recognised, understood and implemented throughout the teaching elements of an academic's work. Appreciating the importance of the three functions will have an impact on how practice may be improved.

To monitor and plan ahead

The type of information and records tutors collect should help the planning of future sessions, schemes of work and programmes of study. It should also help identify specific problems that individual students may have. Planning in this context requires the tutor to build upon previous progress and ensure that they allow the student to progress in an adequate way by covering learning areas in breadth and depth.

To inform others

Records are kept not only to monitor progress of individual students but also to inform a variety of audiences as to the work, progress and problems encountered when teaching a programme. There are four main areas in reporting that the academic needs to be aware of (see Figure 7.2):

1 Reporting to external examiners.
2 Reporting to exam boards.
3 Reporting to students.
4 Reporting to colleagues/departments/whole faculty.

Each requires different skills and use of evidence, but each type of report has to be informed and based on data collected.

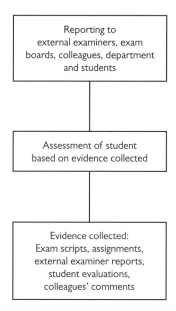

Figure 7.2 A framework for recording and reporting

REPORTING TO EXTERNAL EXAMINERS

At the end of every academic year exam boards are held for each respective programme. External examiners are part of this process. External examiners will expect you to report on any problem student. Many of these reports are verbal at exam boards. However, external examiners might request further information regarding students' progress or extenuating reasons for poor student performance. Such evidence has to be provided. Each department, school or faculty will have in place systems for the nature of evidence to be collected and the processes by which such evidence can be used. It is very important that you familiarise yourself with these procedures prior to any visit or encounter with external examiners.

REPORTING TO EXAM BOARDS

Exam boards and boards of study are part of institutions' internal mechanisms for ensuring quality. It is the responsibility of each programme director to write a report about the progress of the programme, and the number of students it has recruited, retained, passed and failed. Each institution will have a formalised procedure for such events. Reports also have a proforma to follow; these again will have an institutional approach. More senior members of staff will direct you to where and how to write the required reports. Reports for boards of studies and exam boards have different functions. It is important that these distinctions are understood and reflected within the said documents.

REPORTING TO STUDENTS

Every student has the right to know how he or she is progressing. The tutor can achieve this in a variety of ways. Feedback is the key: after an assessment task, communicate to the students what they have achieved and attained, and what they need to do in order to progress further.

REPORTING TO COLLEAGUES

This is a skill that develops with experience. The information collected and recorded in relation to the course and student progress is important, as it informs colleagues of problems that may have been encountered by the student during the teaching of certain topics. The records should be specific, with examples of where and how the student or students encountered problems. Detailed records are a means of monitoring one's own practice in relation to students' learning difficulties or successes.

Summary points for consideration

Assessment allows both you and the students to know how much they have learned and provides a chance for more learning to take place. Assessment should be designed with primary course learning outcomes in mind: they should cover what has gone on in a module, lecture or series of sessions. Before compiling an assessment go over the kinds of information, skills and knowledge emphasised in the course or module. Was the memorisation of facts or the applications of principles more important? The assessment should be constructed to reflect the basis of what was taught and the expectations under which it was taught.

Chapter 8

Revising and improving teaching

Introduction

This chapter focuses on how to review your teaching and how the evidence collected from the review can improve teaching. It will consider the concept of the reflective practitioner and show how this can facilitate effective learning environments. Consideration is given to the responsibilities of the academic to improve teaching in a variety of ways, including their research activities, their own professional development in their discipline areas, as well as keeping informed on the latest teaching methodologies such as ICT (information, communication and technology). Finally, academic professionalism is considered by showing how working through and reflecting on the ever-increasing demands of research, publications and large group teaching can help in meeting these demands.

Teaching improvement

Teaching improvement is something that should go on all the time for all academics. You incorporate a better example or analogy into your lectures, you decide to teach an innovative course or introduce IT in a dynamic way to your discipline. Frequently these changes and improvements are unconscious. However, it is important to become conscious of how and why you change your teaching strategies and methods. There comes a time when change becomes or needs to become deliberate. What is important is that you recognise the need to change and develop your teaching. This can be done in investing in peer observation, critical reflection and a conscious change in approach.

In order to change and become aware of the changes you have to distance yourself as a teacher. Teaching is often considered a very insular and private affair. Often as individuals we are willing to let our colleagues critically review our writing and research, yet we are far more hesitant in allowing our peers to review our teaching in action. Even teachers who ask for peer observation are hesitant and defensive when they hear anything negative about their teaching. Distancing yourself allows you to recognise what teaching skills you have and which skills you may still need to develop and attain.

Whatever steps you take to improve or further develop your teaching skills will benefit both yourself and your students' learning. Good effective teaching is very rewarding both personally and professionally. Students appreciate good teaching, which is often reflected in good work and high attendance.

The role of assessment for the individual

The argument for the role of assessment for the individual has often been associated with its contribution to motivation through the recognition of achievement. Research has shown that the way individuals learn is directed both by personality and motivation (Wittrock, 1986; Berliner, 1996). This research suggests that learners perceive themselves and the way they account for their learning success and failures as having a strong connection to their motivation and performance. In the professional context new and experienced academics involved in the learning process must be given the opportunity to learn how to frame and reframe the complex and often ambiguous problems they face when trying to interpret and modify their practice and behaviour (Schon, 1988).

Schon distinguishes reflection *in* action, which is akin to immediate decision making, and reflection *on* action, which provides a longer and deeper view. Schon gives a perspective on reflection that helps the discussion surrounding assessment. However, it is difficult to think of assessing reflection in action and on action. A different perspective, such as that put forward by Hatton and Smith (1995), is more helpful. They suggest that 'reflection might be defined as deliberate thinking about action with a view to its improvement' (p. 52).

How can this statement help in terms of improving one's teaching? Here reflection must be thought of as a key and essential aspect of self-development. New lecturers should be encouraged and facilitated in the development of the reflective process. Reflection occurs at many levels, and new lecturers should be encouraged to engage with a variety of levels of reflection. Kolb's (1976, 1984) learning cycle provides a useful discussion framework for the development and engagement with the reflective process.

Kolb sees the learning process as being composed of a four-staged cycle. Immersion in immediate concrete experience is viewed as the basis for observation and reflection. Observations are assimilated into an idea, image or theory from which implications for future action may be derived. These implications, hunches or hypotheses then guide planning and implementation of experimental action to create new experiences, to reflect on these experiences, to integrate observations into more abstract conceptual schemes or theories and to use these theories to guide decision making and experimental action to solve problems leading to new concrete experiences.

The useful aspect of the cycle is that it demonstrates that different learning situations fosters different skills. An effective environment highlights experiencing of concrete events; a symbolic environment emphasises abstract conceptualisation; a perceptual environment emphasises observation; and a behavioural environment stresses taking experimental actions. What one needs to develop is an encounter with each element of the cycle. Kolb claimed that individuals' preferred learning styles become more effective the more they reflect the completed cycle. What this cycle allows us to do is capture aspects of learning experiences which can then point to practical implications, including the desirability of maximising the opportunity of any experience to support learning and hence develop both personally and professionally.

What this theory offers is that it explains how learning through a particular experience takes place; it does not however tell us whether the individual can transfer this learning to other situations. This is where a second set of learning cycles would be needed. This second set is essential for additional learning in the everyday environment, which is necessary for the learning to impact on the individual's job performance. Each set of cycles requires reflection, but the second requires critical reflection at a deeper and more meaningful level.

What is it to be a critical reflective learner?

What is it to be a critical reflective learner and how can it be facilitated if development and further improvement in teaching and learning is to occur? Engaging in such processes should become second nature in all aspects of academics' learning and work, whether this be teaching, learning or research.

Being truly reflexive is a capacity that higher education emphasises as characteristics of its being. Reflexive capacity both on a personal and professional level is crucial to the development of the academic within the environment of the higher education institution. Barnett (1997) states clearly that 'reflection and critical evaluation, therefore, have to contain moments of the creation of imaginary alternatives. Reflexivity has to offer resources for continuing development' (p. 6).

Critical reflection of this nature has to be engaged in by academics when they themselves are learners; it is not just essential but a prerequisite to learning and developing. Improving one's teaching requires understanding critical reflection, and engaging with it in an academic and systematic way.

What can be improved? (Figure 8.1)

The argument so far has related to new and experienced academics involved in their disciplines, with teaching, learning and scholarship directly related to that discipline. This suggests that although there are generic qualities and common elements to teaching, learning and scholarship, academics perceive their work as primarily led by their own discipline. Becher (1989, p. 20), summarises the notion of knowledge and disciplines well:

> It would seem, then, that attitudes, activities and cognitive styles of groups of academics representing a particular discipline are closely bound up with the characteristics and structures of the knowledge domains with which such groups are professionally concerned.

Considering the types of knowledge academics might need as professionals helps the discussion. Eurat's (1985, 1994) work suggests that professional knowledge may be categorised in such a way as to help view development. Eurat (1994) distinguishes between different types of knowledge, how they are acquired and their role in professional action. He suggests three broad areas: propositional knowledge, personal knowledge and process knowledge.

Propositional knowledge contains three subcategories:

1   Discipline-based theories and concepts derived from bodies of coherent systematic knowledge.
2   Generalisations and practical principles in the applied field of professional action.
3   Specified propositions about particular cases, decisions and actions.

Such knowledge may be used in one of four ways: replication, application, interpretation or association. Together they account for aspects of disciplined-based knowledge that make up parts of professional knowledge.

Figure 8.1 Areas of possible improvement

The second form of knowledge is described as *personal knowledge*. This is composed of impressions, and knowledge acquired through experience. *Process knowledge* is defined as knowing how to conduct the various processes that contribute to professional action. This can be taken as Ryles' (1944) distinction between 'knowing that' and 'knowing how'. To Eurats' distinctions of types of knowledge he adds that of *professional knowledge*. This, he suggests includes acquiring information, skilled behaviour, deliberate processes such as planning and decision making, giving information and metacognitive processes such as control of behaviour. These categories give us an indication of the complexity of knowledge areas the academic is working with. Candy (1994) adapted and further developed Erauts' three distinctions to produce five areas of skills a professional requires if they are to progress within their given profession. These are:

1   Knowledge skills.
2   Thinking skills.
3   Personal skills.
4   Personal attributes.
5   Practical skills.

For the purpose of this discussion the knowledge skills and thinking skills form the basis of the argument. This is not to say that personal skills and attributes and practical skills are not important; however, in terms of assessment the former two aspects are key elements.

Knowledge skills

Let us consider knowledge skills and how these relate to issues within a given discipline. When referring to teaching this involves what Shulman (1987) calls 'subject-pedagogy' or a 'pedagogy of substance'. 'It involves mastery of that variety of ways (demonstrated by expert teachers) by which the particular concepts of a field are translated (transformed) into terms accessible to and understandable by students at their particular stages of development' (Edgerton *et al.*, 1991, p. 2). Such knowledge is at the heart of a scholarship of teaching (cf. Chapter 6). It is a type of knowledge that is integrally related to the deep knowledge of a discipline and demands a clearly articulated notion of what constitutes knowledge within the given discipline. Taylor (1993) provides us with a description of knowledge-based information that may help in identifying areas for assessment. The analysis put forward considers content (substantive knowledge), problem solving (thinking and reasoning strategies), epistemic norms and values, and modes of inquiry and criticism (pp. 69–70).

Within Taylor's description is the implicit notion that learning occurs. The knowledge base provided by him fits well with Ryles' (1944) 'knowing that' and 'knowing how' concept. These two aspects may be re-categorised into two elements: conceptual knowledge and procedural knowledge. Whereas procedures provide the means to secure goals and sub-goals, concepts provide a conceptual basis to guide the goal-directed activity of problem solving (thinking and acting), as well as goals for performance.

Problem solving is an important element as it is central to securing cognitive development. Both conceptual and procedural knowledge are used in everyday practice to organise activities and secure workplace goals. Procedural knowledge secures goals that concepts provide. An example here is that of a mathematician wishing to introduce the concepts related to higher order calculus. Before this occurs he or she must be aware of the procedures involved within the concepts, as well as the variety of procedures that may be used to teach the concepts. This requires an understanding of both the discipline-based knowledge and what Shulman calls the subject-pedagogy.

Conceptual knowledge is differentiated by levels of complexity or depth (Evans, 1991; Greeno, 1989). These levels range from simple factual knowledge through to more complex levels of conceptual knowledge. The importance here to development is that the richer the association and interconnectedness of the conceptual knowledge, the more likely the individual to transfer their conceptual knowledge. This makes conceptual knowledge significant, as it permits the formulation of goals and assists with the deployment of procedures to secure workplace performance. This type of knowledge and thinking in conjunction with good procedural knowledge allows the experienced and expert academic to analyse problems and offer more effective solutions than novice or inexperienced academics achieve.

Professional development that encourages experienced and inexperienced academics to work together can bridge the gap between the use of procedural knowledge and conceptual knowledge. It is at this juncture that the development of reflective skills is needed. If academics are to translate their discipline-based knowledge into effective pedagogy two things need to happen:

1   They must learn the techniques, rules and guidelines of the different forms of inquiry within their discipline; different elements call for different skills.
2   They must learn about themselves, and what it means to be part of the different elements of their discipline. They must attend not only to the knowledge and skills of chemistry, law or history, but also to themselves as future chemists, etc. within the academic community and the world at large. They must address what it means to have 'competence' in both these areas.

Essential to the above is the understanding of what it means to be reflective.

Reflective skills (thinking skills)

The concept of 'reflection', reflective practice and critical reflective learning has and continues to be an important aspect of professional development. Research has shown (Boud *et al.*, 1985; Burnard, 1995; Kolb, 1984) that reflection on experience can be thought of as a vehicle, through which learning occurs. Hence reflecting directly on professional practice should be a core element of the academic's work. Mezirow (1992) reminds us that 'reflection is generally used as a synonym for higher order mental processes. However, it demands more than drawing on what one already knows in order to act, it requires critical thinking aimed at examining and justifying one's beliefs' (p. 5). This suggests that if academics are to develop their practice, a process including both personal and professional growth, then critical reflection on practice will be central to the learning. Here development is taken as moving beyond the acquisition of new knowledge and understanding into questioning existing assumptions, values and perspectives.

Dewey's (1933) definition of reflection is useful here to take the discussion forward. He considers reflection as 'active persistent and careful consideration of any belief or supposed form of knowledge in the light of the grounds that support it and further conclusion to which it tends' (p. 9). What Dewey is referring to here is the need for individuals to learn to think, by being able to 'discriminate between beliefs that rest upon tested evidence and those that do not' (p. 97). This process may be summarised as when individuals think, they delay action until they:

- Understand the situation thoroughly.
- Know the goals they want to reach.
- Consider as many options as possible for reaching that goal.
- Assess the options they have.
- Make a plan before taking action.

Dewey's view is that being able to discriminate between those things that are beliefs and those things that are based on evidence are 'critical factors in all reflective or distinctively intellectual thinking' (1933, p. 11). This type of reflection is closely linked to Mezirow's notion of critical self-reflection, and key to changing and developing the individual. Essential to all these definitions of reflection is that the individual is the key participant, a participant who understands what it is to reflect and be involved in the reflective process.

If reflective learning is to impact on the quality of teaching, learning and scholarship we as an academic community need to be clear as to the aims and purposes of the process we are being asked to engage in, especially in relation to the demands of the ILT. Clearly, if reflection is to be part of an overall assessment strategy it must take account of generic and discipline-based knowledge and skills. Assessing the process of reflection, reflective dialogue and critical reflective learning needs to be addressed differently if it is to be an effective tool for development within the academic community. Critical reflection is central to the process of transformative learning and change, but not all critical reflection leads to transformation and change; we can question and inquire without having to change things. For transformative change to occur the process of reflection has to involve and lead to some fundamental change in perspective and consequent action.

Personal reflection often evidenced in the form of a self-report or reflective narrative is the only evidence that may be produced to show change, development and learning. Assessment of such evidence needs to place value on self-reports and critical narrative, but at the same time must ensure reliability, coherence and clear criteria for the assessment.

Reflection and reflective learning are key aspects to improving one's teaching and learning. The documentation of such reflective practice is the evidence collected and exemplified for such improvement. As such, a reflective portfolio (cf. Chapter 11) should demonstrate the following elements:

- The way critical reflective learning in terms of outcomes within a discipline is identified.
- The way reflective dialogue has taken place and been ascertained (with peers and colleagues).
- The way evidence of the learner's participation in the dialogue is established.
- The way evidence of a developmental process over time, regardless of the start or end point, is identified.
- The way evidence of the review system that enables an understanding of the learning process has taken place is recorded
                    (Modified from Brockbank and McGill, 1998, p. 102)

If evidence of reflective learning is used constructively it can demonstrate Mezirow's three types of reflection that lead to transformation and change. These are *content reflection*, *process reflection* and *premise reflection*. The nature of this evidence may be found in:

- learning review;
- review records;
- reflective commentary or narrative;
- reviewer and peer reports.

What constitutes the three types of reflection suggested?

Content reflection

Content reflection produces the type of reflection advocated by Dewey (1933). It allows individuals to reflect on the content or description of a problem; i.e. it facilitates individuals to 'learn how to think, and discriminate between beliefs that rest upon tested evidence and those that do not'. For example, if an academic has a problem with integrating their research into their teaching, the academic might look for indicators of appropriate and inappropriate points within the module or curriculum to introduce the research and link them closely with effective teaching strategies. If the academic then notices that the research is being better understood and applied successfully by the students, the academic might then wish to develop the strategies further to incorporate more research into their teaching. This type of reflection can help the academic perceive their work within the context of their discipline, and change their pedagogic practice through concentrating their reflection on their research and scholarship.

Figure 8.2 shows the nature of possible steps taken to achieve change. Within each step identified in the diagram, evidence relating to reflection, planning, research and teaching can be documented and recorded.

Process reflection

This stage of reflection relates to thinking about the strategies used to solve the identified problem, rather than the content of the problem itself. Here the academic might ask whether or not the routes chosen to find indicators for integrating research into their teaching were adequate. The questions they should be attempting to answer are:

- Are the indicators relevant?
- Are the indicators dependable?
- Are the indicators transferable to other situations?
- Are the indicators helpful to solving the problem?

Figure 8.4 shows how the reflective process incorporates process reflection into the original example, allowing the individual to consider how to think

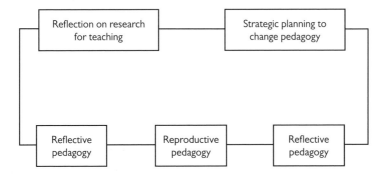

Figure 8.2 Examples of content reflection

about the original problem and to establish how far they have gone towards solving it.

Premise reflection

Within the context of teaching, learning and scholarship this might well be the most important aspect of reflection. By that I mean it is assisting in asking the question, 'What is the relevance of the problem itself?' In our example the question would relate to relevance of trying to integrate recent research into teaching. The academic might wish to approach this issue by asking the following questions:

- Is integrating my research into my teaching my concern and responsibility?
- Should my research be integrated into my teaching?
- Is the integration of new research findings a valid approach to teaching?
- Are my research findings of any relevance to my teaching?

These questions are crucial for academics to understand and be aware of. Premise reflection allows the individual to examine the assumptions under which their beliefs and values underlying the problem are being questioned.

In essence, critical reflection by the individual should allow them to see the expectations they have of themselves, their students and their role in an academic community. If this is the case, the reflective academic can begin to question and examine these assumptions and become free to choose to revise them if they are found to be distorted, unreliable or invalid.

Perceiving the academic as a critically reflective practitioner and learner casts doubts on the merits of attempting to assess reflection as a means of enhancing the quality of teaching and learning. The premise of this statement lies in the fact that creating the critical reflective academic is not a matter of improving techniques, but rather a process of engaging them in understanding why they do what they do. If the academic truly engages in reflective practice, a consequence of this action will be a 'real change' in practice based on articulating the assumptions underlying practice, realising the consequences of those assumptions, critically questioning the assumptions and, as Barnett says, 'imaging alternatives' to current perspectives and practices.

Using reflection for improvement

How can the new academic become a critical reflective practitioner who engages with the process of reflection as a means of improving teaching and learning? In order to reflect it is essential that one must have something to reflect on, as such evidence is a key prerequisite. What this evidence constitutes and how it is collected is also part of the process of improvement.

Consider the cycle shown in Figure 8.3. The five steps can help improve your teaching in the following way:

Asking the question

Defining the question related to your learning and teaching is the starting point to engaging with the process. Identifying your knowledge or skills gap is a skill in its own right. The way in which you frame your question related to practice is fundamental, as it helps to identify and clarify the problems you think you may have as well as providing the type of information you may need to change and improve your practice. You will need to think around three or four elements, such as:

1   What is the problem – the students, the subject area, your pedagogy or traditional practices?
2   What interventions or changes are you considering or planning and why?
3   Are there any alternative interventions or changes you could employ or consider?
4   What outcomes are you looking for?

For example: A group of students are found to be demotivated, and will not respond to questions or interact in sessions. You need to decide whether your teaching methods are creating this behaviour or it is how this particular group behaves all the time. The pedagogic question might be:

> For this student group (problem) would a change in pedagogic practice (intervention) compared to no change (comparison) increase their responsiveness and motivation to teaching sessions (outcome)?

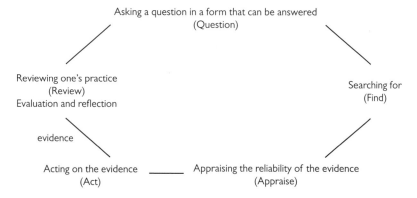

Figure 8.3 Reflecting and reviewing cycle

This question focuses on the nature of change and the types of interventions that might be implemented as a means of improving teaching and learning outcomes. This leads on to the next step, which is to find the relevant supportive evidence.

Finding the evidence

Consider first the problem and identify if any other members of staff have similar problems with the group/topic/session. It may be that you are not alone in your identified problem. If it appears that the problem is yours, try to identify what this is by talking to the students, and asking them to fill in an evaluation form following your sessions. You could also ask for a peer observation, so an independent observer can give you feedback on the issues. The evidence they provide will help you to explore other areas for improvement, such as literature in the field, staff developers or colleagues within your school, faculty, or department.

Appraising, evaluating and reflecting on the evidence collected

The nature and content of the evidence you have collected regarding your teaching and student learning will be specific to the questions you asked in relation to the identified problem. The next step is to appraise that evidence. Appraising the evidence should help you to decide three things:

1   Whether you can trust the evidence you have collected.
2   What the evidence means.
3   Whether the evidence is relevant to your situation.

To appraise these three areas critically you have to be honest with yourself with regard to the evidence collected, how it was collected and what the evidence is saying. Systematic review is crucial. There is no point asking students to talk to you and evaluate your performance if you then cast aside their comments.

A systematic review of your performance should address the following questions:

- Is your evidence valid?
- What is the overall evaluation of your teaching saying?
- How precise are these comments and issues?
- How can the evidence help you to alter your practice?
- How will you use the evaluations and evidence to reflect on your practice?
- What strategies do you need to employ based on your reflections?

The final question should lead you to posing new questions in relation to the improvements you hope to implement within your teaching. Figure 8.4 shows how the process of asking questions, monitoring and systematic critical review will help obtain and analyse the evidence to improve practice.

Points for consideration

Use the above questions to develop an action plan and reflections of your teaching.

The above steps are aimed at helping the individual engage in the process of reflective analysis as a way of learning from practice. Brockbank and McGill (1998) suggest that academic staff who engage in critical reflective practice have one of the key tools for their own learning and development. As teachers adopt an approach that promotes the kind of learning that is envisaged as appropriate to learners in higher education they will have within that approach a basis for their own continuing professional development (p. 99).

The process that the teacher engages in (i.e. that of critical reflection) should become intrinsic to their role as teachers, thus involving themselves in their own professional development. Such reflection and development then becomes intrinsic to improvement of pedagogic practices.

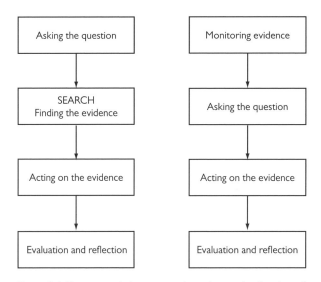

Figure 8.4 Process to help systematic review and reflection of pedagogy

Taking pedagogic practice forward

Understanding and applying critical reflection is, as explained above, key to improving teaching skills and understanding the reasons why things have succeeded or failed, need modification or complete change.

Equally important to the process is understanding why evaluation and reflection should even concern us. The first issue is to recognise that to take pedagogic practice forward there is a distinction between finding out that something is not working in your teaching sessions and why that something is not working. The first gives you a set of facts much like research adding to a body of knowledge, while the second provides information for decision making. This, while the comment 'even if the results/facts about your teaching are not utilised' its redeeming feature is its intrinsic value and contribution to your knowledge about your teaching capabilities. However, this may well give you information, but it is inappropriate for critical reflection. In short, for improvement to take place it is important for the individual to 'need' the information about their teaching as well as 'care' about the information about their teaching. In this way they can engage with the 'why' issues and use the information to provide pathways for action. The whole process is justified by its contribution to the rationalisation of decision making.

When engaging in the process it helps to think of why the 'why' issue has to be engaged in. Are you trying to understand why your teaching skills need improving because:

- You want better evaluation from students for their own sake (window dressing)?
- It is necessary to pass probation (external requirements)?
- To maintain your reputation within your school/faculty or department (public relations)?
- Professional and personal prestige (personal development)?

Attempting to be reflective as a window-dressing activity is unlikely to improve your pedagogic practice in reality. Using reflection in this way merely gives justification for decisions you have already made about your practice, hence there is no real engagement with critique.

Reflection that is used to maintain compliance with external requirements, such as induction programmes or probation boards, is also not the way to improve practice. If the individual feels that the primary goal of the board or programme is to hear only positive aspects of pedagogic practice, it is obvious that is what the individual will produce, irrespective of any serious problems in other areas of one's practice. Here reflection becomes solely a pro-forma exercise to meet the needs of the board or programme, and an exercise which does not engage the individual in real improvement and development.

Reflection that is used as a public relations exercise is equally futile. If reflection is perceived as a gesture to demonstrate the objectivity of one's teaching strategies by the fact that they appear to be successful to the rest of the department is not the means to personal development. What is important here is that in the 'eyes of the school/faculty or department the teaching is good', and not the potential learning outcomes of that teaching.

The last category of professional and personal prestige is one that highlights the type of reflection which engages the individual in such a way that both professional and personal development occurs. It recognises the 'why' issues. It pays attention to the fact that the individual is in a constantly changing environment, where new actions are being taken all the time, some for the good, others for the bad, but each action is taken for a reason. Critical reflection in this context demonstrates one's own recognition and awareness of the actions taken and the ensuing changes as a consequence of the actions taken. It also allows for an articulation of why the changes happened and their overall effect. This type of critique involves learning both of a personal and professional nature. It is also the type of reflective activity towards which the professional educator should strive.

Points for consideration

Using the four categories of window dressing, external requirements, public relations, and professional and personal prestige, identify which category you operate in and why.

When thinking about improving teaching it is helpful to consider the notion of the 'concept' of what good teaching at higher education level might constitute. Research by Reid and Johnstone (1999) suggests that there are six components to the concept of good teaching. These components were derived from discussions with students and tutors from a variety of settings in higher education. What is interesting about these components of teaching is that it breaks down elements of teaching and learning in a way that can encourage the individual to look at specific areas. Table 8.1 shows what Reid and Johnstone call 'construct taxonomy'

Some of the criteria used to identify the concept of good teaching were as follows:

Approachability	positive	• friendly and approachable
	negative	• not always available
Clarity	positive	• gives adequate explanations
	negative	• hard to follow
Depth	positive	• good knowledge of underlying theory
	negative	• superficiality of academic knowledge

Interaction	positive	• creates supportive classroom dynamics
	negative	• no student participation
Interest	positive	• uses variety of teaching aids
	negative	• stale, recycling familiar information
Organisation	positive	• well organised
	negative	• not as well thought out as it should be

Table 8.1 Construct taxonomy

		Staff
Approachability	• Approachable • Sensitive • Humiliates students	Promotes interaction and deep thought/ distant and detached from students. Exceptionally good knowledge of underlying theory/lacking theoretical knowledge/powerful experience base.
Clarity	• Lucid	Practical understanding combined with diverse theory. Competent/restricted to narrow field and unwilling to talk outside it.
Depth	• Depth of treatment • Research • Contributes • Questioning attitude	Effect on students – gets them buzzing with ideas. Challenging but not off-putting. Gets them to question own assumptions and ideas/no sense if getting students to think about assumptions. Delivery of content in decontextualised way. Models not critically assessed. No development of theory of epistemological thought. Experiential and innovative learning – individuals thinking at pinnacle. Deep learning.
Interaction	• Students actively involved • Participation encouraged	Internalised – intrinsic motivation. Facts and theories developed in response to students' thinking/opposite. Exam orientated, formalised traditional, rote-learning. Depth of academic knowledge/superficiality of knowledge.
Interest	• Interesting • Entertaining	Superficial statements that appear to have great weight/difficulty in being superficial or sloganistic.
Organisation	• Organised • Varied method • Use of technology	Element of superficiality/depth. Depth of insight residing in practical framework or realistic construct/no or limited evidence of such insight.
		Students Display of theory/reflective. Updates lectures all the time; material all recent.

The results of the research show that staff rank interactions above that of approachability and that students reverse this ranking. Students rank 'interest' above 'depth', with a reverse ranking for staff. Students rank clarity higher than staff.

What this clearly shows is that if one wants to improve one's teaching it is important to consider both your own position and what students perceive, think and feel. Consider the first reversed ranking: interaction and approachability.

As a lecturer, it is clearly important to interact with the students, and interaction is a key element of good teaching, but if you are not approachable to your students it is unlikely that they will interact with you. Interaction is important to students; however, research suggests that students place greater importance on the interest of the topic, the lucidity of the presentation and the approachability of the lecturer.

In order to improve teaching it is necessary to consider not only the evaluations of your teaching from peers, students and yourself but also to consider your preconceived ideas of teaching in relation to the evaluations you have obtained. The reason for this is two-fold: (1) it allows you to reflect on why you have approached your teaching in the way you have; and (2) it allows you to reflect on what and how you could change your teaching.

Research evidence (Brookfield, 1991; Prosser and Trigwell, 1997; Reid and Johnstone, 1999) has clearly demonstrated that teachers' preconceived ideas about teaching influence their practice. When challenged and asked to review these conceptions a more reflective-based approach to teaching is developed. Reid and Johnstone (1999) have shown that during the reflective phase lecturers redefined the importance of interaction, depth and clarity.

How can this research help in reflecting on one's teaching? First, it identifies areas in which new lecturers can focus their attention, and second, it directs one to reflect not only on preconceived ideas of teaching existing practices. Consider again the element of interaction. Interaction has been an important aspect of pedagogy for a long time (Dewey, 1933). Lecturers often place interaction with students high on their list of good teaching. This reflects lecturers' desire to empower students. Giving students autonomy for their own learning is after all an aim of higher education: however, students are not always as comfortable with such an approach as those who advocate the process. Lecturers should try to establish where on the continuum of learning their students are. Bouffard *et al.* (1995) showed that teaching self-motivated, confident postgraduates using interactive methods is very successful; however, for new, less-experienced students it is not so successful. Hence the concept of interaction needs to be thought through in conjunction with the student population that is to be taught.

Approachability

How approachable do you perceive yourself to be to students and how approachable do you think students perceive you as? As lecturers you are constantly in your department, teaching, researching and socialising with students and peers. It is therefore easy to perceive oneself as very approachable. This is not necessarily what students consider as approachable. You need to be available to your students academically whether through tutorials, extra help or e-mail. Students need to have confidence in asking for help and direction; this is an essential entitlement for student learning. However, this approachability needs to be put into a context of time and manageability. Here ground rules as described in Chapter 4 are essential. Insist on appointments or timetables of events, but do allow students reasonable access. To improve teaching, approachability and interaction need to be considered together. As Reid and Johnstone (1999, p. 278) suggest.

> The two dimensions of interaction and approachability are seen to negate each other . . . if student empowerment for their learning is a function of interaction, then the student concept of approachability, which might rest more in a view of the teacher as guardian and transmitter of tradition, could be legitimately perceived by staff as undermining the empowerment process.

Clarity and depth

As a new lecturer it is essential to have both clarity and depth within your teaching. As stated above, it is interesting that students look for clarity first, then depth. When starting out in lecturing it is easy to assume that students hold a certain body of knowledge, and as a consequence your lecture starts from a point of specific knowledge and goes into further depth through the course of the session. Clarity will help the explanations, but if students are lost due to not having the prerequisite knowledge, depth becomes irrelevant. To improve teaching it is important to ascertain prior knowledge of students (cf. Chapter 4). Then plan the content and depth of knowledge for your teaching sessions. If clarity of explanation and delivery is added to the equation, a good teaching experience should ensue for all.

Interest and organisation

Gaining the students' interest is very important to good teaching, but does not require you to perform great tasks or feats of entertainment. Interest can be gained through a variety of situations and processes. Being superficial or sloganistic is not the answer. Being well organised, aware of your students' attention span and being realistic about your teaching are more important.

A well-organised and structured teaching session which includes a variety of methods and short activities will keep students interested and motivated. Improving your organisational skills is an essential element to success (cf. Chapter 4, Planning framework).

Changing your practice

In order to change your practice and improve your teaching you have to be aware of and be prepared to challenge your own perceptions of strength and weakness in your teaching. Whatever your concept of good teaching, it may not necessarily be reflected in your actual pedagogic practice. Improving your teaching requires you to question your practice and critically reflect on what that practice is and how it might change, be improved or strengthened further.

Points for consideration

Identify your perceptions of good teaching. Use these to find evidence of how successful you are, and reflect on that evidence.

How do you know your teaching has gone well?

There are many indications of successful teaching: student response, evaluation sheets and peer review. However, these are not always available and necessary for each session that is taught. So how can one evaluate the success of one's teaching strategies?

Tables 8.2, 8.3 and 8.4 respectively give some suggestions and criteria against which evaluation of teaching may be measured.

Lecturers who take account of the criteria given in Table 8.2 will find ways to reflect and hence improve their teaching sessions. Tables 8.3 and 8.4 shows some of the elements that need consideration with respect to effective teaching.

Table 8.2 Criteria for evaluating teaching

Teaching quality is judged to be good by the extent to which:
- Lecturers have clear aims and learning outcomes for their teaching session
- Students are aware of these aims and learning outcomes
- Lecturers have a secure command of the subject matter being taught
- Teaching sessions have suitable and achievable content
- Teaching activities are well chosen and are focused on promoting learning outcomes
- Teaching tasks are presented in ways that engage, motivate and challenge all students, allowing individual learning and progress to be made

---

Table 8.3 Elements of effective teaching

The students:
- Clearly perceive the purpose of the teaching session
- See a practical application for what has been learned
- Solve real problems
- Actively participate in the process of learning
- Become autonomous learners
- Develop skills and acquire knowledge
- Discuss their work
- Derive enjoyment and satisfaction from a job well done and realise that these are related to the amount of work they put in
- Learn from their mistakes
- Receive constructive assessment of their efforts from teachers and fellow students
- Perceive their own progress and development
- Change their ways of thinking about the subject

Table 8.4 Elements of effective teaching

The teaching:
- Has a clear purpose and a strategy for achieving it
- Is firmly structured with a beginning, a middle and an end, yet with the possibility of being varied to take account of opportunities which arise unexpectedly
- Takes account of students' prior learning
- Takes account of differences in students' ability
- Offers a variety of teaching strategies
- Challenges students' perceptions and ways of thinking
- Generates a dynamic and motivating atmosphere which allows students to become involved and achieve
- Demands high standards
- Provides a learning environment that encourages students to participate and actively learn

Concluding points

Developing and improving teaching skills is a key aspect of every lecturer's professional development. This chapter has stressed the need to be able to reflect and understand critically the nature of reflection. The various tables and figures have given examples of the issues, criteria and questions one needs to ask if such reflection is to occur and thus improve teaching. Teaching skills can be acquired and checked relatively simply, but establishing student learning is not quite so easy. Building your professional knowledge and judgements in the areas related to student learning, teaching styles and professional judgement is key to effective teaching. For teaching to improve and enhance student learning the lecturer must understand the principles of the cycle of critical reflection, as it is this cycle that will produce the evidence required to reflect critically and make progress.

Chapter 9

Leadership, management and administration

Introduction

Leadership, management and administration are all part of an academic's life. Many of the tasks associated with these three roles are not ones that the new academic is essentially accustomed to or even familiar with. However, each has to be cultivated, developed and implemented at various stages in one's career. So how do new academics deal with and develop these skills? This chapter aims to help and facilitate in these three areas by defining what each term means for the academic and how each of the elements may be developed and nurtured.

Leadership

What is leadership and how can it be developed? Leadership is to do with how people relate to each other. Leadership is about learning (Ramsden, 1998). A working definition of leadership can be taken to be 'Leadership as influencing the behaviour of an individual or team'. It is about accomplishing goals through the efforts of other people and not doing things yourself.

Elements of academic leadership

Ramsden (1998) suggests a simple model of academic leadership (Figure 9.1) that is useful to help structure both the new and experienced academic's approach to leadership issues.

Ramsden suggests that core academic leadership responsibilities are represented by the middle block and are twofold. Leadership is first about producing excellence and second about a focus on change and innovation that harnesses traditional academic values.

Academic leadership must provide the means, assistance and resources which enable academic and support staff to perform well. Leadership is about:

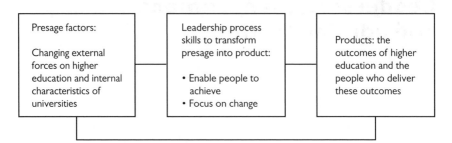

Figure 9.1 Elements of Leadership

- Producing excellence.
- Focusing on change and innovation.
- Harnessing academic values and strengths to meet new requirements.
- Tensions and balances.
- Inspiring and energising others to achieve.
- Effectiveness.
- The ability to consult and listen.
- Creating trust.
- Understanding chaos and bewilderment.

> **Points for consideration**
>
> If you take charge of a project, what leadership skill might others look for in you and how can you ascertain if you possess these elements? Consider some of the points below.

Effective leadership is characterised by four elements:

1 Purpose, direction and meaning.
2 The ability to generate and sustain trust.
3 Optimism.
4 A bias towards taking action and achieving results.

(Jones, 2000)

These four elements may be considered in terms of a major research project one undertakes for the first time. What will other members of the team expect from the project leader and how can this be attained? Team members will expect the project leader to:

- Have a clear vision of how the project is to perform.
- Have the ability to capture their imagination in relation to the project work.

- Instil belief in the team that they can perform to their full potential and achieve a successful outcome to the project.
- Have a clear focus.
- Have the autonomy and trust to achieve the goals in a way best suited to the teams skills and knowledge.

Good leadership skills within a project, department or larger responsibility framework require the individual to have a vision that is clear, attainable and attractive to those whom they are to lead. Team members must feel they can share the beliefs, goals and vision set down by the project leader or department head. Clear thinking, strategy and vision instil confidence in those who are required to perform the tasks of meeting goals; it must also instil trust in that these goals are accomplishable as an individual and a team.

Generating and sustaining trust is a key element if leadership is to be effective and efficient. Jones (2000) suggests that trust is:

- The 'social glue' that binds individuals.
- One of the key factors that enthuses individuals to do things to achieve results.
- Based on the confidence the individual has in the competence of the leader.
- The product of openness of the leader and the ability to create empathy with all the team members.

Trust is therefore an element that any new leader must establish with his or her team. What then will team members expect from their leadership in terms of trust and the sustaining of that trust?

Points for consideration

The questions below are aimed at making an individual think about the key elements regarding trust and leadership. Use them to help you consider your own position as team leader.

- How can you develop empathy with your team?
- How can you ensure you see the project in the same way as your team?
- How can you establish consistency in your behaviour and expectations during the project?
- How will you establish your integrity?
- How will you demonstrate your standards, expectations and ethics?

Any project or team work will have its high and low points. One of the key elements of a good leader is to have and demonstrate optimism for the work or development being conducted. Optimism may be demonstrated in a number of ways, including:

- Showing commitment to the vision of the future of the project or development.
- Not dwelling on mistakes and problems but seeing them as opportunities to learn.
- Respecting and celebrating the diversity in a team as a benefit to all.
- Inspiring and enthusing those within the team that goals are obtainable despite setbacks.
- When things go wrong being prepared to listen to the team and to be optimistic for a successful turnaround.

Leadership is not just to do with certain qualities such as trust, optimism and clear thinking; it is about achieving goals and targets successfully. Producing results is a measure of success. A good leader will always have these targets and goals at the back of their minds, as well as constantly reappraising the situation in how to achieve the set goals and targets. For this to occur a leader needs to:

- Provide the drive to convert the purpose of the organisation and team into action.
- Give a clear vision and purpose that provides results.
- Enable people to see results by which they can measure their own and their team's achievement.
- Translate the vision and goals into action: this requires having a plan to implement the vision.
- Demonstrate success and show a serious commitment to success.
- Demonstrate a drive and desire to succeed.

Points for consideration

Below are points that individuals quote as wanting from leadership. How do you think you can respond to such comments?

- He or she knows exactly what is wanted at any specific time.
- He or she has a passion for the goals we are aiming for.
- He or she gives us a clear picture of what our goals are.

Many of the elements discussed above will come with experience, some will come naturally and others will have to be learned. Every academic aspires for promotion and the opportunity to lead their own research and teaching team. To do this requires a multitude of skills from expert knowledge to publications and teaching excellence. However, there are some basic points that all potential leaders need to consider when thinking about leadership, the most significant element being what will leadership be measured against and what are the basic criteria on which others will judge the leadership.

Most will look for the following in a successful leader:

- *The development of team spirit.* Everyone in the team should have a sense of alignment that is an understanding of shared objectives to which they are dedicated.
- *Making a difference.* Team members will feel that they are at the centre of things and everyone will believe they can make a difference to the success of the organisation, project or development.
- *Learning culture.* All individuals will feel they are encouraged to learn from their experiences and are not afraid that all their mistakes will be punished. They feel that they have the power to find problems and solve them.
- *Evaluating leadership.* The team should be encouraged to evaluate the leadership. This evaluation should be formative so that the leader can learn and develop. Reflection on leadership skills is a key aspect of good development of leadership.

Point for consideration

To be an effective leader requires an understanding of one's:

- Strengths
- Weaknesses
- Beliefs
- Areas of development
- Ability to reflect
- Obtaining feedback
- Being open to learn
- Being aware of one's own values and ethics.

Use the above points and Ramsden's conceptualisation of academic leadership (Figure 9.1) as a means to establish your strengths, weaknesses and possible areas for development.

Management

What is management? Management is a focus on efficiency, on systems, control, procedures, policies and structures and the status quo. Basically management is about 'doing things right'. It differs from leadership in that leaders produce change; effective leaders produce 'constructive or adaptive' change to help people and firms survive and grow. They establish direction, align people, and motivate them. Leadership is about 'doing the right thing' (Ramsden, 1998).

Within the university setting there is a belief that firm, fair and efficient management which gets things done effectively is different from inspirational leadership but equally desirable. So what then is expected of the good manager in higher education?

It is possible to look at what tasks are given to managers and leaders to highlight what is expected. Kotter (1990, p. 139) compares the tasks related to management and leadership. He suggest that there are four areas in which the comparison occurs. These are:

1   The creation of agendas where a manager plans and budgets but a leader sets directions.
2   The development of human networks, where a manager organises staff but leaders align people and groups.
3   Execute the agenda, where managers control and solve problems and leaders motivate and inspire.
4   Impact, where managers create order and leaders produce change.

Kotter's distinction between management and leadership in relation to academic people and academic work (Figure 9.2) shows how we can begin to describe what may be expected from an academic leader and an academic manager.

There are four areas for consideration. What is most important to the discussion here is the lower quadrant, which focuses on management. This

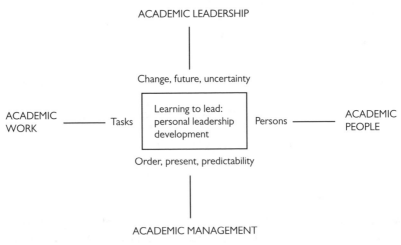

Figure 9.2 The domains of academic leadership

Source: Ramsden (1998, p. 125).

lower quadrant may be further divided into two. The first relates to academic tasks, including planning and budgeting, quality assurance, and effective administrative processes. The second relates to the management of people with a focus on supervision of staff and their efficient organisation through selection, delegation, rewards and performance management. It is these elements that have to be mastered if efficient and effective management is to occur.

The sets of tasks have been divided into two. It is necessary to consider each set separately with regard to project planning, a task that all new academics have to deal with very early on in their careers. Knowledge of these tasks is frequently assumed by more senior and experienced academics.

Planning, budgeting, quality assurance and effective administration of a research project

Planning may be regarded as having three stages, each of which is interlinked but at the same time needs time spent on it individually. Each stage contains a set of statements and questions to guide the planning and implementation of a research or development project. The nature of the statements and questions will also help to accumulate the relevant evidence to document the project you are responsible for.

Stage 1. Initial project framework

- Establishing what needs to be done is set in place and processed. Many of these issues will be derived from the aims and objectives of the project outline or proposal.
- How will what needs to be done meet the expectations of the funders or project stakeholders?
- How will the project be conducted?
- Who will conduct the project, and will they be accountable and responsible for it?
- If it is not the same person, how will they be line managed and how will their performance be monitored?
- What are the resource implications?
- What is the project budget and how will it be managed?
- Who will be responsible and accountable for the project budget?
- What is the timetable for the project and how will this be managed against staff time?
- What mechanisms need to be established in order to ensure that the project is effective and has met its aims and objectives?

Stage 2. Monitoring and target setting

- What mechanisms need to be put in place to ensure regular monitoring of the project?
- If there are many members of the team should the team be subdivided; if so, how, and how will they report to the main project leader?
- How will meetings and reporting be structured?
- Are there to be interim reports; if so, have they been included in the main project timetable?
- How are the finances of the project to be monitored?
- What contingency plans need to be put in place in case things go wrong?
- How will the findings be reported to the appropriate bodies and how will they be verified?

Stage 3. Conclusion

- What evaluation mechanisms are required?
- Evaluation has to be on several fronts: project wide, individual performance, financial and results/findings.
- Performance indicators need to be explicit.
- Successes and failures need to be recorded and referenced.

The above stages are a basic framework by which a project may be planned, monitored and evaluated. Writing a proposal is only the first step to successfully completing the research project. The above stages are given as a guide to structuring and thinking about issues related to academic planning and monitoring. Preparation in these areas will make a significant difference to the management of the project and its successful outcome.

Managing academic duties

Increasingly, new academics have to manage and be responsible for programme development in some form. Whether this is a single module or an entire degree programme, the responsibilities are considerable. Many questions unfold around the issues of programme development, most of which relate to course content and are dealt with in Chapter 5. However, there are other equally important issues that need addressing when managing programme development and delivery.

Managing a programme requires planning, preparation and organisation of resources: human, financial and structural. It also requires an appreciation of student body and staffing expertise. When managing a programme or developing a new programme the following should be taken into consideration:

- Human resources/academic expertise.
- Level of programme/student body.
- Managing and monitoring student learning.
- Finance.
- Accommodation/consumables/resources.

The nature of the programme that is being developed will determine the questions that need to be addressed regarding human resources. Some examples are given below.

Human resources/academic expertise

- Will the programme be a single module or a complete degree programme?
- If a single module, will you be teaching and marking the module?
- Does the single module fit into an established programme? If so discuss with other members of the programme how your module best fits, and what the implications are for them.
- If a complete programme, how many staff are required to develop and to teach the programme? Are the developers to be the same as those who teach the modules within the programme?
- How will you organise staff developing the programme to come together to produce a coherent programme?
- How will you establish the academic expertise for the programme? Do you have the relevant staff? If not will you buy in and have you the financial resources to do this?

Level of programme/student body

The level of programme being designed and developed will have an impact on the staff required and the quantity of academic material that has to be developed. The following questions will help in determining the nature and context of the student body at which the programme or module is being aimed.

- Who is the module or programme aimed at?
- At what academic level is the programme to be developed?
- How will you ensure appropriate academic level?
- What will the students be expected to do in terms of attendance, assessment and compliance?
- Will the students be full-time or part-time or both?
- Will the students be undergraduates or postgraduates?

Managing and monitoring student learning

Managing and monitoring student learning has become a key element of academics' work. This process has to be both efficient and effective as well as meet quality assurance standards and procedures. When developing a module or programme, managing and monitoring student progress and learning must be a high priority.

Student learning has been dealt with in Chapter 3; however, here it is more important to consider the management issues related to that learning and progress. Managing and monitoring progress should be designed and built into any programme or module being developed. It is important to consider the following questions when designing the programme:

- What quality assurance processes have to be followed in order to meet school, faculty or university standards?
- How will these quality assurance processes be monitored?
- What type of assessment will students have?
- How will assessment be monitored, recorded and feedback made to students?
- How will standards across the programme be monitored, reported and recorded?
- How will progression through the programme be monitored?

These are fundamental questions that need to be managed and dealt with at the inception of the programme or module.

Finance

Increasingly, financial viability of programmes is a key factor to keep them running. It is therefore essential that the following points are considered when developing any programme or module:

- How will the programme be resourced?
- What are the full-time equivalents (FTEs) you are working to?
- How many staff do student numbers allow you to budget for?
- Are the projected student numbers adequate to sustain the programme?
- Are any other departments involved, and if so how are they to be financed?

Many of the financial questions will require assistance from the relevant finance officer within the department, school or faculty. However, it is important that an understanding of programme finance is achieved in order to develop resources and implement a programme.

Accommodation/consumables/resources

Programmes or single modules will all require accommodation and resources varying in nature. It is essential that the nature and context of the programme or module being developed takes account of existing room facilities and resources that are available or might need to be acquired specifically for the programme or module being developed. These consumables or resources can have a significant impact on the viability of a programme financially and in terms of human resources. If the expenditure outweighs the return financially the programme may not run. Equally, if the programme is designed for a certain level of expertise and this is not available, the programme will be of poor quality. The following points should be considered:

- What types of room will the programme require?
- How often will the programme require these rooms?
- Will the room accommodate all the students comfortably or will more than one room be needed?
- What consumables will the programme require and in what quantities?
- How many extra staff are required to make the programme functional and are they available to the programme?
- Does the module or programme require any additional resources; if so what are they?

Points for consideration

Use the above descriptors and the Ramsden model of leadership as a way of identifying your leadership skills, potential and possible strengths and weaknesses.

Conclusion

Good leadership skills come with time. They are skills that need to be practised at all levels and at all times. This chapter has aimed to introduce the basic concept of leadership, management and administration. Increasingly, higher education is expecting more from its academics. This requires a variety of skills to be demonstrated across a broad spectrum of activities. This chapter has introduced some of the key issues such as leading a project and programme development. As time goes on and more responsibility is given, leadership and management skills will also develop.

Chapter 10

Continual professional development

Setting the context for professional development

Chapter 1 considered the role and implications of the ILT with respect to teaching and learning. It is now necessary to examine the role of professional development within the context of the ILT and higher education more generally. This chapter gives a description and overview of the role, concepts and issues related to professional development in higher education. It discusses the relationship between learning from learning, different ways of learning and knowing and professional development. It gives a framework for planning one's own professional development and shows how institutional development and individual development need to be considered carefully and sympathetically.

Professional development has many aspects and facets to its name. Within higher education much of the discussion relates to learning, whether this be lifelong learning, organisational learning or discipline-based learning. Higher education concentrates on learning, both of the students and the academics. It is therefore right and fitting that the fundamental premise within this chapter is that professional development is closely allied to the learning cycle. From this premise consideration is given to the impact and influence professional development approaches may have within institutions and the impact these have on the individual. These include administrative procedures and commitments to programmes, support networks from institutions and senior colleagues, and resource implications.

What is meant by professional development?

Professional development is a dynamic process that spans one's entire career in a profession, from preparation and induction to completion and retirement. This view is based on the assumption that any successful professional development relies on a relationship related to the individual's work environment and their perception of their role within it. Figure 10.1 shows

Figure 10.1 Relationship between professional development and the individual within
            an institution

Source: Entwistle and Ramsden (1982, p. 200).

the relationship between professional development and the individual
within an institution.

Central to this conceptualisation of professional development is the
position, and the effect of each of the constituent parts on the individual.
It is important for this discussion to consider each aspect, then to move on
to how these aspects affect and are linked to notions of learning and
professional education.

Professional learning and learning from learning

Professional learning is a key aspect in any discussion related to professional
development. Work by the Carnegie Foundation, and in particular Ernest
Boyer, has drawn particular attention to professional learning within the
academic community. Boyer (1987) suggested that 'All faculty members,
throughout their careers, should themselves, remain students. As scholars
they must continue to learn and be seriously and continuously engaged in
the expanding intellectual world' (p. 10).

For university academics, it is the case that contact with the teaching and
learning situation on an almost daily basis has always contributed to the
development of higher education academics' academic and pedagogic knowledge and skills. This being the case we can assume that practitioners have
been involved in personal development and learning by the nature of their
position and job. Equally, professional development is part of learning, and
studying the subject and related issues is a privilege for those involved in
education and educational studies. Yet in a learning society we are forced to
ask questions relating to professional development and its role in learning. A
consequence of the Dearing Report has been the need for the higher education sector to consider and enter the debate about learning from learning
and how this equates to scholarship. It is suggested here that 'learning from
learning' is a key facet of development. This point is strongly argued for by
Becher (1996). In this context professional development is seen as having its

central concern with the promotion and support of learning, not only for the students but also for the academics themselves in their own personal and professional development.

Research has shown that the ways in which teachers think about teaching substantially influences the approaches to learning adopted by students (Prosser and Trigwell, 1997). Research has also shown that academics' view of the nature of knowledge and the relationship of that knowledge to their teaching influences the extent to which they are prepared to innovate, and learn from their teaching (Brew and Wright, 1990). If learning is taken as a process of construction (Biggs, 1996; Entwistle, 1997; Prosser and Trigwell, 1997), as being about the creating of knowledge rather than simply absorbing it, then an alternative perspective can be given to the academic learning from their research and teaching.

The concept of learning may be viewed as developing a personal understanding of a phenomenon, in this case teaching, research, scholarship and the links between them. The implication of this is that teaching needs to take account of how individuals develop their conceptions as well as the conceptions that are being developed. Key to this argument is that the academic has to understand that the relationship between teaching and research is dynamic and context driven. What is important to the argument is that if such a process does not occur, then that individual is not engaged in developing and learning. This would suggest that if academics are to be learners, and learning is given value, then learning opportunities that provide access and progression (in this case to teaching/learning programmes through professional development) have to be actively and reflexively engaged in. Edwards (1997) quite correctly emphasises that there has been a shift in focus from the provision of education as training to one that focuses on the learner and learning. Thus he argues that the discourse of lifelong learning has shifted to one of reflexive challenges; one that requires the professional to learn and understand the learning that has taken place. This perspective is clearly laid out in the ILT's proposed national framework for continuing professional development.

Continual professional development: a national framework

The ILT's national framework for continual professional development (CPD) sets out clear criteria and expectations of the nature and quantity of CPD academics have to engage with. The suggested framework is still under consultation as this book is being written. There has been significant discontent with the nature, context and content of the suggested framework. It will be interesting to see the final outcome of the consultation period.

The document sets out a considerable amount of prescription within what constitutes CPD, as well as the outcomes expected from engagement in CPD activities. The terminology used is forceful and directive, introducing terms such as professional competence, conformity, outcomes, required documents and obligation. How can this be interpreted within a community as diverse as higher education, where many if not most academics are involved in CPD through their discipline-based societies or learned bodies? What does it mean for academics to 'remain in good standing'?

From an ILT perspective this requires academics to keep a personal professional development record (PDR) to support teaching. The principles underpinning this development record are:

- The systematic updating and planned improvement of professional competence throughout an individual member's working life are necessary to support career progression and to respond to changing work environments.
- While ILT members are responsible for deciding on the precise means by which they meet the requirements to remain in good standing, the character of CPD activities may be influenced by institutional policies and practices.
- Members have a professional obligation to maintain currency both in their specialist subject area(s) and in the pedagogy of that subject; to demonstrate this commitment ILT members should present their evidence in an accessible format which allows for easy scrutiny.
- The ILT has a duty to assure itself, the public and other bodies that its members adhere to the requirements of the national framework in terms of their professional competence and conduct; as such it will establish mechanisms for the periodic verification of its members' professional development records.
- The ILT has a responsibility to provide best practice guidance on CPD to its members and to support their professional development.

The underlying principles of the framework are expanded by describing the need for appropriateness of CPD activities, and these 'collectively' will enable members to demonstrate convincingly that they 'remain in good standing' with regard to their professional standing. Evidence is to be drawn from:

- professional work-based activities;
- personal activities outside work;
- courses, seminars, conferences and training events;
- self-directed and informal learning.

An average time of forty hours would be required by the ILT to satisfy CPD guidelines.

The stated demands are clear and specific in the sense that they are prescriptive and appear to be definitive in their requirements. Yet there is ambiguity about what might constitute evidence and the proportion of personal and professional documentation required within a portfolio of CPD.

What is presently problematic with the proposed CPD is that the guidelines are inappropriately over-specific as to the forms of evidence required. What is required from CPD is evidence that individuals have developed both breadth and depth in the work they do as teachers. It is also important that members demonstrate that their standing be maintained in respect of their pedagogy within their subject.

The required documentation for CPD starts with the statement:

> The Institute accepts and strongly endorses the need for an appropriate mix of subject-based and pedagogical elements in members' professional development records. Such elements should clearly reflect the different roles, contexts and teaching responsible of individuals and documentation should normally contain a range of evidence drawn from a variety of sources.

Examples of such evidence may be collected from a variety of sources including descriptions, evaluations, and reflections on formal and informal learning aimed at maintaining, updating and upgrading knowledge, expertise and professional practice. Requirements state that the professional development records (PDR) should place emphasis on outcomes and the application of learning. Below are some of the suggested types of admissible evidence:

- evaluated activities aimed at the improvement of learning methods and teaching performance;
- action research and evaluation of individuals' own teaching and assessment methods;
- examples of the development of new learning resources or innovative curriculum design;
- relevant management/leadership activities of direct relevance to learning and teaching (e.g. preparation for subject review, mentoring of new academic staff).

The above examples are outcomes led and 'focus' on what Barnett (1996) has termed 'the distinction between pragmatic results and cognitive offerings'. A similar argument may be made about critique. One of the expectations of the national framework is that individuals will engage in a significant amount of reflection within the five broad areas that are demanded by the ILT. These are:

1   Planning and preparation;
2   Conducting teaching and learning sessions;
3   Assessment and evaluation;
4   Reviewing and improving teaching;
5   Academic administration, management and leadership teaching.

The main aim of the CPD requirements is to maintain good standing within the professional body of the ILT by demonstrating professional competence and the enhancement or extension of professional competence, through reflection on evidence collected. The use of reflective techniques is intended to bring about greater effectiveness in learning and teaching through a better cognitive understanding of the processes involved in teaching and learning (cf. Chapter 11).

The aim of this form of CPD is to gain more than an operational understanding of 'greater effectiveness'. As an academic teacher there is a need to know more than when things work or do not work in a learning environment; one needs to know why they have worked or not worked. This relies on understanding the concepts, ideas and theories that are related to various aspects of teaching and learning within a given discipline.

The reflection needs to demonstrate understanding of the reasons why operational success or failures occur. Barnett's distinction between operational and academic reflection helps in identifying the type of evidence that is required. He states:

> academic critique is reflection orientated towards understanding better the already existing understanding. On the other hand, critique in the operational sense is an understanding that enables us 'to go on' with greater confidence.
>
> (Barnett, 1996, p. 166)

At present this well describes the type of reflection the ILT expect from portfolio material: the type of reflection that shows improved performance based on outcomes.

Issues, role, concepts and practices of professional development

Professional education may be considered as being concerned with three main aspects of development, namely the professional knowledge base, competence in professional action and the development of reflection. Yet one of the paradoxes of professional education is that practitioners are encouraged to develop a critical awareness of the context of their practice. This awareness includes the problems of their clients, whether this be patients or students, while at the same time the notion is perpetuated that the professional practitioner is an autonomous free-thinking agent. If this is the case one has to ask the question: *How do practitioners learn their practitioner role?*

This is a pertinent question to ask when entering higher education, particularly when statutory requirements related to the development of learning and teaching skills are being imposed on the academic practitioner. A practitioner who may consider himself or herself as a research chemist, psychologist or economist by definition, in the first instance, not a teacher as yet, is being asked to be an excellent teacher practitioner.

Determining your professional needs

Professional development is about learning and modes of learning. At present most modes of professional development in higher education are shaped by the social structures in which they are located and by the influence of historical traditions of learning. So why should academics develop their knowledge in relation to teaching and learning, and be motivated to become 'good teachers'? Personal and institutional influences affect the academic's motivation to participate in professional education activities. The transaction between the individual and the external factors contributes to a state of motivational energy to engage in continual professional development. The factors that affect academics' participation can be grouped into personal or situational categories. Much of the research in this area suggests that reasons for participation or lack of participation can be aligned with personal factors, factors that contribute to and influence academics' level of motivation. Rowland (1998) highlights the issue of motivation in relation to the pressure for academics to embrace the notion of good teaching

Practice, in this case teaching, does not happen in a vacuum. It depends on a variety of social, political and ideological contexts. The practice of teaching in higher education and the role of learning for the academic are equally dependent on the whole educational context, particularly at this point in time when universities are facing periods of rapid change. For these reasons, understanding one's strengths and weaknesses is key to future development. Thus, every academic has to continually review his or her learning and developmental needs, both generic and discipline based.

The development of a reflexive professional is a long-term process, one which is progressive and spans the working lifetime of that professional. It is planned and prioritised.

Points for consideration

In relation to your present position consider the following questions:

- What does competence in teaching and learning in your discipline or subject area mean?
- What are the competencies required by your discipline?
- How can these competencies best be developed in your discipline?
- How proficient are your competencies within your discipline?
- How can you improve and what do you need to improve?

The need for continual professional development

There are many reasons for considering professional development as an important part of career development. When new into the world of academia, skills related to teaching, learning and research develop constantly within discipline knowledge and pedagogic practice. However, it is essential that these skills continue to be developed. Planning for this is key, not simply to meet statutory requirements but as a means of remaining an effective academic. The most important reasons for planning and engaging in future development include:

- Extension of experience in a particular way (e.g. special educational needs, the use of ICT in teaching and learning).
- Development of professional knowledge and understanding in certain areas (e.g. transferable skills, assessment, effective management).
- Extension and development of teaching skills in a particular element of your discipline or specialism.
- Developing skill of writing policy documents.

Professional development falls into two categories, that of personal development and institutionally led development. It is important to appreciate that the two are inextricably linked, and that overall individual and institutional development cannot occur in isolation from each other. This has recently been written about as the learning organisation, one which takes the view that 'if institutions are about promoting the learning of students in a changing world and learning is worthwhile and not about a static or bounded process, then the learning of education professionals throughout their careers is essential' (Craft, 1996, p. 11). This suggests that as academics it is important to accept the fact that we have to continually learn in order to cope with the increasing demands for change within the higher education sector. It is therefore necessary for all those involved in higher education to understand and engage in professional development.

What is professional development?

Continual professional development (CPD) is about enhancing and extending knowledge, pedagogy and experience. It is a significant part of academic development; it is also a way of enhancing effectiveness as a researcher and teacher, and thus gaining promotion through a developing career. CPD is the process by which academics may explore existing skills, knowledge and responsibilities, and endeavour to maintain, enhance and transfer these skills to a variety of situations that occur in the academic community. This can be achieved by considering your starting point and where you want to go in the future. Professional development involves self-review, target setting and individual planning.

Any institution will expect to see development in all areas of competence from their academics. It is the academics' responsibility, with the help of the institution, to be involved in the type of professional development that facilitates that development. For many new academics the starting point will be the expectations laid down by their probationary board and their head of faculty or school. The starting point for planning future development will be set by these expectations. Evaluating the situation is key. Consideration of the following points will help focus discussions and planning related to future needs and expectations.

Points for consideration

- What areas of development arise from my probationary board?
- What other areas do I want to develop?
- What is your preferred style of learning?
- What personal areas do I want to develop to help my career path, research, curriculum development, management or administration?
- What do I want from my appraisal in terms of specifying development needs?

A combination of all these factors will influence the context of any involvement in continual professional development. Figure 10.2 summarises the interplay of issues that could help in planning professional development activities.

Figure 10.2 Interplay of issues in planning professional development activities

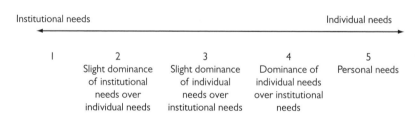

Figure 10.3 A continuum of needs

Source: Bolam (1995).

Professional development: the individual vs. institution

Professional development may be considered from a variety of perspectives, many of which have more recently been structured into a number of models and frameworks. Bolam *et al.* (1995) identify five basic areas of consideration based on a continuum of learning that meets both the individual and institutional needs. At one end of the continuum the individual's needs dominate and at the other the institution's needs dominate; this is shown in Figure 10.3. Within the institutional needs he includes:

- staff/group performance;
- individual job performance;
- career development;
- professional knowledge;
- personal education.

Bolam's model allows us to consider how professional development can be directed towards the individual and the institution. What does this mean in terms of the new academic trying to progress? If we consider the continuum and regard (1) as dominated by the institution this could be an induction programme on learning and teaching. The focus of these sessions would require specialist input or discipline-based workshops. At the other end of the continuum we may consider (5) whereby the individual academic is concerned only with their own personal growth. This may involve training in a grant application specific to their field, or engaging in a Ph.D. or post-doc research of their choosing. If the institution is to gain and the individual to develop, there needs to be collaboration between institution and individual.

Bolam's model allows both the individual and the institution to be viewed together and individually. The implication of this is to understand and recognise the difference between individual and institutional needs.

Development needs to include:

- Making people feel valued for the job they are involved in.
- Enabling people to do their job well and receive feedback that is essential for job satisfaction and motivation.
- Helping individuals to anticipate and prepare for change within their working environment.
- Encouraging individuals to derive excitement and satisfaction from their involvement in change.
- Making individuals feel willing and competent to contribute constructively to the development of the institution.

The above points recognise and identify areas in which both individual and institutional needs have to be addressed if effective learning and improvement is to take place. It is this issue that is still causing a dilemma in developing effective professional development initiatives in higher education.

It is important here to consider the individual and the institution. Figure 10.4 attempts to show how collaboration is needed between the individual and the institution if they are both to learn and to grow. The underlying assumption is that collaboration between the individual and the institution is needed if joint development is to be successful, sustained and evolve in the future. The central starting point is the individual and the institution. The example used is the induction programme for learning and teaching within higher education.

The top half of Figure 10.4 represents external and internal issues of direct relevance to each in their own right. Individuals are primarily involved in their own research and scholarship, and are responsible for the teaching and learning that takes place within their remit. Their teaching and learning activities are monitored by the school/faculty or department and are subject to peer observation, the outcomes of which have to be dealt with by the individual. Overall the individual is measured against quality outcomes.

The higher education institutions are primarily involved in educating adults and responsible for research of a higher standard. As such, research is expected to raise the the quality of the courses provided. Both research and teaching quality are externally inspected and audited, thus giving the quality

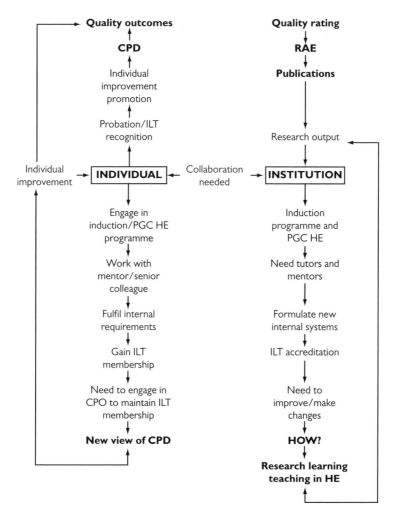

Figure 10.4 Need for one-to-one collaboration

and rating of an institution. Although the above descriptions are simplistic they are similar in content but differ in context. Both are constrained by external and internal outcomes and ratings.

If professional learning and development is to occur through each stage, as individuals and institutions are introduced to new scenarios, what are the binding commonalities and how can these influence professional development? Teaching, learning, research and quality outcomes is the key. Research helps to bring about development both in the individual and the institution, but there must be a constant interaction between the research taking place and the development of courses and projects that fuel development. It must be seen as empowering the individual and the institution to make fundamental changes in their practice.

Conclusions

Continual professional development (CPD) is an aspect of one's career that cannot be ignored. In higher education, CPD is most often concerned with the individual's subject area, but, as this chapter has demonstrated, CPD has and is becoming increasingly expected within the subjects' pedagogic practice. The nature and quantity of such development has to date not been specified; however, there is an expectation that all academics will be involved in CPD with respect to teaching their subject. For new academics the process of CPD in the areas of teaching and learning is now compulsory. To maintain professional standing in the area of teaching and learning it is important to keep up to date. A starting point can be getting in touch with your subject support centre. There are twenty-four learning and teaching support networks (LTSNs) in the United Kingdom. Each are designated to the development and support of a specified discipline area.

A CPD plan for your career is always a good start. Where you are and where you want to be in the short, medium and long term are key aspects of your development profile.

Chapter 11

Collecting evidence and building a portfolio

Introduction

Teaching portfolios consist of a collection of evidence of teaching and related skills associated with the role of a teacher. They are now required as a part of assessing a teacher's competence in a formal programme of training in teaching and learning in higher education. A portfolio should also be considered as a personal record of achievement, development and personal reflection of one's teaching. A key element of any teaching portfolio is the evidencing of progression in competence. Through the portfolio you collect materials documenting your strengths and accomplishments as a teacher. Peter Seldin, author of *The Teaching Portfolio* (1991), says, 'the portfolio is to teaching what lists of publications, grants and honours are to research and scholarship'.

What is a teaching portfolio

A teaching portfolio is a factual description of lecturers' teaching strengths, accomplishments, and areas of development. It includes documents and materials that collectively demonstrate the scope and abilities of a lecturer's teaching performance.

The contents of a portfolio vary, depending on the capabilities and course responsibilities you may have. Typically, however, portfolios include a personal statement, supporting material from others including peers who have observed you, evaluations from students in relation to your teaching effectiveness, videos of your teaching, and any innovations in teaching you may have developed, used and evaluated. A portfolio-mapping tool is described in Table 11.1. Use this to help develop your portfolio of evidence for submission for ILT membership.

Why a portfolio of teaching?

In the busy life of an academic it is quite justified to ask why a portfolio of teaching? A portfolio of teaching should be seen more than just the requirement of membership to the ILT or for the purposes of a probationary board. A portfolio can serve as a reference point to:

- Provide structure for self-reflection about areas of teaching needing improvement.
- Demonstrate how teaching has evolved over a period of time.
- Demonstrate how effective teaching has been through the collection of student evaluations, peer review, etc.

A portfolio can be a source of evidence of one's development for a variety of reasons. However, it is also important to state that a portfolio is not an exhaustive compilation of all documents and materials associated with one's teaching performance. Instead, it should demonstrate a selected set of information on teaching activities and how effective these activities have been. Brockbank and McGill (1998, p. 103) suggest that a portfolio is a:

> Compilation of learning intentions, accounts of learning activities, learning outcomes, records of reflective dialogues. It includes evidence from a variety of sources including your private learning journals/diary/ log and most important of all, a reflective document detailing your learning process. The ... portfolio, while confidential to you, is intended for assessment. And therefore you will need to consider what to include/exclude and adopt a style, which is appropriate for others to read who may not have witnessed the event or process.

What should a portfolio contain?

The portfolio should provide evidence of teaching and teaching-based experiences/practice. It should contain evidence of teaching observation, student evaluations, and methods of assessment and course design and evaluation. The main purpose of this material is to help develop one's personal reflection and learning in teaching in higher education and to provide evidence for assessment of a range of teaching practices at professional level. At a reflective and critical level, this evidence should integrate personal experience, relevant knowledge/theory and the values and principles of academic practice. As such, a portfolio would be expected to contain:

- Documentary evidence showing a wide range and depth of teaching practices.
- Knowledge of the relevant literature and key concepts/issues of practice.

- Practical understanding of the relationship of practice to the relevant literature and values.

The portfolio is a highly personalised product; there is no prescribed way in which it should be structured. However, a portfolio will be expected to address the academic principles at the centre of whichever programme the portfolio supports. Different fields and courses cater to different types of documentation. For example, developing teaching strategies and materials for an introductory economics course is significantly different from preparing a graduate seminar in organisational theory or a freshman's biology course. The items chosen for the portfolio will depend on the teaching style of the lecturer, the purpose for which the portfolio is being prepared and the level of critical reflection that is going to underpin the portfolio itself.

A portfolio is based in principle on empirical evidence gathered by the individual lecturer as a means of showing teaching development and competence.

Principles of academic practice

When portfolios of evidence were first thought of as desirable for the assessment of teaching competence in higher education, the concept of academic principles was thought important. These principles were considered important to teaching in higher education and were expected to be demonstrated by new lecturers, which were underpinned by the following professional values:

- a commitment to scholarship in teaching, both generally and in the discipline;
- a respect for individual learners and for their development and empowerment;
- a commitment to collegiality;
- a commitment to ensuring equality of educational opportunity;
- a commitment to continual reflection and consequent improvement to practice.

(From Accreditation and Teaching in Higher Education Planning Group, Booth Committee, 1998.)

Collecting the evidence

Most of the material you will require for a portfolio can be divided into three broad categories. These have been adapted from Seldin 1991.

1 Materials from oneself

- Statement of teaching responsibilities, including course titles, numbers of students, enrolment, and a brief statement about whether the course is required or elective, graduate or undergraduate.
- A reflective statement by the lecturer describing his or her personal teaching philosophy, strategies and objectives, methodologies.
- Representative course syllabi detailing course content and objectives, teaching methods, reading, self-directed study material.
- Participation in programmes on developing and enhancing instructional skills.
- Descriptions of curriculum development, innovation, including assessment of their effectiveness.
- Involvement and development of student assessment procedures.
- A personal statement by the professor or senior colleague describing teaching goals for the next three years.
- Description of steps taken to evaluate and improve one's teaching, including changes resulting from self-evaluation, time spent reading journals on improving teaching.

2 Materials from others

- Statements from colleagues who have observed your teaching in the classroom.
- Statements from colleagues who have reviewed your teaching materials, such as course content, programme development assignments, assessment and grading practices.
- Student course or teaching evaluation data which produce an overall rating of effectiveness or suggest ways to improve.
- Honours or other recognition from colleagues, such as distinguished teaching or student support awards.
- Documentation of teaching development activities through the university staff development centres.

3 The products of teaching/student learning

- Students scores on pre- and post-course examinations.
- Examples of graded students work along with your comments as to why they were so graded.
- A record of students who succeed in advanced study in the field.
- Student publications or conference presentations on course-related work.
- Successive drafts of students' papers along with your comments on how each draft could be improved.

- Information related to students' career progress based on the impact of your course or support.

4 Other evidence that is often submitted in a portfolio of teaching

- Evidence of help given to other lecturers leading to improvement in their teaching.
- A videotape of your teaching session.
- Invitations to present a paper on teaching one's discipline.
- Self-evaluation of teaching-related activities.
- Participation in off-campus activities related to teaching and learning.
- A statement by the head of school or faculty, assessing your teaching contribution to the school or faculty.
- Description of how computer, films and other non-print material are used in your teaching.
- Contributing to, or editing, a professional journal on teaching your discipline.
- Performance reviews as a faculty member.

When compiling the portfolio it is important that you meet the demands of those who are to assess the document. The above suggestions are based on what might be included and should be used as a guide. Being selective is the key to success. It is important that you build a picture of how you have developed your teaching skills based on evidence which should be included in your portfolio. Of equal importance is how you bring together all this information. The best approach is through your reflective commentary.

Integrating the items in a portfolio

A well-constructed portfolio integrates the documentary evidence and material collected from one's self and one's colleagues in a manner which clearly demonstrates competence in teaching and effective student learning. It should also demonstrate willingness to continue to develop in the areas of teaching and learning in your discipline. The portfolio should offer a coherent teaching profile in which all parts support the whole. For example, a statement regarding your philosophy of teaching might reflect an emphasis on scholarship in teaching while most of the materials you have put forward as evidence reveal a complementary focus on scholarship through rigorous library assignments (Seldin, 1991, p. 4). Table 11.1 shows how evidence collected from your teaching may be mapped in such a way as to meet the requirements of the ILT and the academic principles and values suggested by the Booth Committee.

Points for consideration

Using Table 11.1 construct an action plan for collecting and structuring your portfolio of teaching evidence.

What can a portfolio demonstrate?

As already suggested, a portfolio of evidence will be a collection of material that is particular to the individual. However, in the collection of this material coherence is required. In order to establish such coherence the following questions need to be addressed:

- Does your evidence show a change in your perceptions of teaching and learning?
- Does your evidence and commentary demonstrate knowledgeable reflection, thoughtful analysis and creative presentation?
- Does your evidence represent understanding and intellectual growth in the pedagogic demands of your discipline?

These questions will help direct the nature and description within the portfolio. The portfolio should be taken as a tool for promoting reflective

Table 11.1 Evidence in constructing an action plan

Learning objectives/outcomes	*Evidence*
Student learning Understanding students' learning and its integration in practice. This will include both: • a knowledge of the key concepts and theories of student learning; • an understanding of current conceptions, approaches and styles of teaching and their relationship to student learning.	This might include notes/documents/plans (with appropriate justification and rationale) re: • individual learning differences, learning styles and approaches to learning; • learning difficulties such as dyslexia; • study skills, habits and patterns; • individual differences in student motivation and orientation to study; • multicultural/cultural differences in learning approach and relationships between teacher and student; • how adults learn, especially from experience; • supporting a deep approach to learning; • encouraging the development of knowledge and skill in adult learners; • promoting active learning; • developing students as lifelong learners; • encouraging the development of appropriate relationships between theory and practice, such as problem-based and work-based learning.

The design of a course/ programme/module (from an outline, document or syllabus). This will include:

- aims and objectives;
- teaching strategies;
- assessment strategy;
- evaluation strategy;
- student learning needs;
- relationship to a wider; programme/degree;
- the learning environment and culture.

This might include notes/documents/plans (with appropriate justification and rationale) re:

- the intended learning outcomes of the course;
- a determination of the appropriate content for the course including workload, etc.;
- an understanding of student learning needs;
- an examination of the overall design with reference to the student group and the resources available;
- learning resources (including handouts or workbooks, audio or visual or computer-based materials, for use by teacher or students);
- a course directory/handbook or outline for students which includes the above information, details of assessment, and any other institutional information and guidance.

Teaching and learning methods
Practice of an appropriate range of teaching and learning methods which may include:

- presentations, lectures, demonstrations;
- groups, seminars, projects, teams;
- tutorials, one-to-one supervision;
- practicals (labs, fieldwork, etc.);
- communication and information technology (C&IT).

These will include a range of strategies, e.g.:

- participative;
- problem based;
- games/simulations and exegesis;
- team teaching;
- varying teaching methods and structures.

This might include notes/documents/plans (with appropriate justification and rationale) re:

- teaching plan/script
- teaching notes
- copies of visual aids
- peer observation
- student feedback
- self-assessment
- student work
- establishing and maintaining an appropriate supportive learning environment
- stimulating intellectual curiosity and fostering enthusiasm
- listening carefully to students
- structuring and presenting information well
- designing, selecting and using appropriate
- learning resources and C&IT
- monitoring and reviewing the selection and use of learning resources and C&IT

This will include detailed observation reports of appropriate practical teaching sessions, with appropriate reflective analysis of the issues and learning outcomes.

Student assessment
Design of an assessment strategy. This should include an effective use of and appropriate range of assessment schemes/ methods to support student learning and to record achievement and address both summative and formative methods.

This might include notes/documents/plans (with appropriate justification and rationale) re:

- overall assessment strategy for the course;
- development or selection of assessment methods, questions and tasks;
- development of assessment criteria and marking schemes;
- implementation of the assessment scheme;
- interpretation of the assessment;
- provision of a feedback strategy to students including time frames, content, quantity, style, accuracy, relationship to objectives;
- student evaluation of the assessment/feedback.

Learning objectives/outcomes	Evidence
Support to students The provision of support to students, including appropriate feedback on academic and pastoral issues.	This might include notes/documents/plans (with appropriate justification and rationale) re: • acting professionally within the institution's policy on pastoral and academic guidance; • acting as a personal tutor and guiding students towards appropriate sources of support within the institution; • maintaining and using sensitively a current register of support services provided within the institution; • reviewing students' progress with them; • negotiating and working within professional boundaries.
Evaluation of teaching • Evaluation of own teaching practice with a range of self, peer and student monitoring techniques. • Improving practice and incorporating relevant research, innovations and best practice.	This might include notes/documents/plans (with appropriate justification and rationale) re: • selecting or devising methods for obtaining feedback from students, peers and other major stakeholders where appropriate; • obtaining and analysing feedback; • using the analysed feedback to inform the planning of future practice; • identifying change in the external and internal environment (e.g. discipline developments, policy, resource changes, student population changes), and implementing teaching and learning methods and resources which respond appropriately to these changes; • publications on teaching and learning.
Team work Recognition of one's role within a team of colleagues and the effective performance of academic, administrative, management and research tasks.	This might include notes/documents/plans (with appropriate justification and rationale) re: • identifying with working colleagues (including the administrators who support the course); • establishing and maintaining appropriate working relationships; • identifying and taking initiative/leadership with colleagues (when appropriate) re academic administration and institutional and departmental policy and practice; • acting professionally within this policy and practice.
CPD Reflection on one's own personal and professional practice and development, including the assessment of future needs and the elaboration plans re CPD. This might consist of: • reflection in groups; • private study; • taking appropriate courses.	This might include notes/documents/plans (with appropriate justification and rationale) re: • identifying one's own professional development needs in the institutional and departmental context; • planning appropriate CPD; • undertaking CPD and using this to inform future practice.

| Network
Development of appropriate
support. These might be:
• internal to the HEI;
• external;
• departmental;
• national;
• discipline based;
• cross-discipline based. | This might include notes/documents/plans (with
appropriate justification and rationale) re:
• membership of groups with a focus on professional
  development;
• internal or external internet. |

Source: Adapted from *The Institute of Education University of London Handbook.*

practice (Bork, 1987). If this is the case, the portfolio allows the individual to initiate a dialogue around teaching and learning, as well as evidence of the achievement of that teaching, learning and development.

It is important to realise that the process of constructing a portfolio and the product that finally results might well represent two different things. The evaluator will read the portfolio as an end-product and give it merit in its achievement. What is important to the writer of the portfolio is the process of creating the portfolio, as this embodies the growing pains you will have experienced while developing through your various teaching and learning programmes, as well as the variety of teaching experiences you will have encountered and engaged in. The process of development will reveal most to you as to how and in what ways you have developed as a teacher.

The construction of a portfolio may be thought of as a social practice (Darling, 2000). Here practice refers to a complex human activity governed by rules, standards of excellence that are considered in the light of certain virtues and initiated through a particular intention or set intentions (MacIntyre, 1984). Practices are associated with two sets of parameters: those directed at internal practice and those aimed at external practice. Both sets of parameters are very real and both can be important to those engaged in practice. What does this mean in terms of demonstrating development of practice?

First there is a need to consider the internal parameters of practice. These include such things as the pride that comes from accomplishment, and the pleasure that comes from engaging in certain sorts of activities skilfully and successfully. In order to appreciate such achievement it is important to 'get inside the practice'. This requires understanding that each practice has its own internal structures. The aspects internal to structures are such elements as when an experiment works well and can be replicated to the same degree of accuracy, or when an artist meets the challenge of colours.

External aspects to the practice are such things as rewards, prizes, grades and recognition, namely aspects that are bestowed on a practitioner subject to the judgement of other persons, such as peers and employers (Darling, 2000).

Internal and external goods have an impact on the nature and context of designing a portfolio. It is essential that internal and external contexts are explored and taken account of. As MacIntyre (1984, p. 190) suggests:

> A practice involves standards of excellence and obedience to rules as well as the achievement of goods. To enter into practice is to accept the authority of standards and the inadequacy of my own performance as judged by them. It is to subject my own attitudes, choices, preferences and tastes to the standards, which currently and partially define practice.

Darling (2000) suggests that goods internal to the practice of portfolio construction are much harder to attain and appreciate than goods external, as these are increasingly associated with both process and product. If this is the case a portfolio must also be seen in the light of a learning tool. This will enable the individual constructing the portfolio to learn as well as meet external criteria of assessment.

Learning from the portfolio

The portfolio is in essence an instrument of assessment, and as such it should provide feedback of a type that demonstrates the developments in learning, anticipated learning needs and levels of progress during the period the portfolio represents. It is through this feedback that the individual learns (Butler and Winne, 1995). As I have said above, the portfolio is a learning tool that should give insight into current and potential levels of performance and possible alternative learning routes. A portfolio is aimed at enhancing the learning process by identifying strengths and weaknesses in performance, and developing an awareness of competence and resolution of discrepancies between external standards and achieved performance (Winsor et al., 1999).

Portfolios, if constructed well, have the ability to capture achievements under realistic circumstances and record them. Utilisation of the information used in a portfolio is an essential element of the learning process. It is possible to think of the portfolio as a learner-defined report on the professional growth in competence attained over a period of time. It is used as a document in and alongside professional practice for integrating evolving thoughts and actions and is directed by personal goals and learning needs.

In conclusion, a portfolio and its construction may be thought of as a learner's tool for one's own development and actions. It should show action taken and the basis on which such action has been taken.

Chapter 12

Final discussion

Introduction

The preceding chapters in this book have considered both generic and specific issues related to learning and teaching in higher education. A variety of perspectives and contexts have been given to show that teaching and learning requires a flexible and open approach, as well as an understanding of how students learn and the theories of learning and teaching lecturers take into the teaching situation. I will conclude with a personal reflection on how I have tried to develop awareness towards learning and teaching, as well as individual and academic development.

Summary of the learning teaching context

In the introduction to this book I suggested that teaching and learning have become the focus for increased student achievement. In order to facilitate this increased achievement new lecturers are expected to have an understanding of what is involved in teaching, how students learn, and how they themselves learn from their teaching by reflecting on their practice. The government has been pushing the need for increased teaching skills through the Dearing Report, which ultimately has led to the inception of the Institute for Learning and Teaching (ILT). The concept and inception of the ILT have been a well-meaning and significant attempt to raise the profile and status of teaching and learning within higher education. But in the rapidly changing world of higher education, what are the prospects of the ILT and the role new lecturers will play within it? I have written elsewhere at length about the pros and cons of the ILT (Nicholls, 2001). Here it is sufficient to raise the issues in terms of the role the ILT can play for new academics.

The ILT represents an accrediting body that in essence assesses and monitors the development of academics, with reference to their abilities or perceived abilities in the areas of learning and teaching. It must be recognised that within a climate of completion rates, shrinking funds, increased student numbers and the need to keep research ratings up, it is increasingly difficult for the new academic to develop, improve and sustain teaching quality as prescribed by the ILT. Here it is the role of institutions to facilitate the growth and development of teaching and learning skills within the new academic.

New academics have a great deal of pressure put on them to perform in their disciplines. This usually means gaining research funds, publishing, administering and teaching to a high level of competence, and on arrival to a new position. For some this might be the first time they have had to teach and face a group of 100-plus students. One could say this is a very daunting experience. Increasingly, institutions are trying to approach the areas of teaching and learning so that new academics have the opportunity to develop. Such situations are in their infancy but are growing in number. Institutions should try to develop an environment that encourages academics to talk about their practice, share the good with the bad and increase awareness of the issues surrounding teaching and learning, whether this revolves around teaching groups of 100-plus or giving an individual tutorial.

New academics will be involved in teaching and learning courses within their institutions, thus giving them the opportunity to engage with a variety of perspectives, and facilitating the academic to develop a form of critical reflection that engages them from both a disciplinary and interdisciplinary perspective. Key to the whole perspective of critical reflection is the way in which academics come to understand and share their ideas about learning. It is equally important for them to examine their understanding of the nature of learning (drawn from their own discipline and theories of learning) and how this relates to their practice as teachers and learners.

Learning is thus a fundamental aspect of the academic's armoury. Perceiving one's own learning as coming from that which is taught helps the academic to understand the issues related to learning and teaching difficult topics and concepts to students. Placing learning at the centre of one's development can help clarify how each element of an academic's life can come together. This is demonstrated in Figure 12.1.

When learning is placed at the centre of professional development it gives the academic an alternative approach to plan their development both from a personal and institutional perspective. Throughout this book the aim has been to encourage development in areas of teaching and learning through

Figure 12.1 Learning at the centre of professional development

the engagement of practically based tasks as well as understanding the underlying principles and theory behind the tasks.

The first chapter concentrated on the changing context of learning and teaching in higher education. This is important, as it has had a significant impact on the new academic's entry into the higher education context. As I have already summarised, this has also had a profound impact on the way individuals need to consider how they wish to develop and where they perceive their learning needs to be. Much of the debate has concentrated on raising student achievement. This theme is taken up in the remainder of the book through a pragmatic approach to the skills associated with teaching and learning and underpinned by the theory related to it.

Summary of the development of learning and teaching skills

The book has taken a pragmatic approach to teaching and learning. Often the world of education is so jargon laden that it inevitably alienates academics from reading further into topic areas such as theories of learning and pedagogic practice. Where possible, jargon has been avoided and a clear and simple path to understanding given.

The development of teaching skills, knowledge of pedagogic practice, and the understanding of student learning takes time. Throughout the book I suggest that essential to the development and understanding of teaching and learning is the process of reflection, a type of reflection that is meaningful and critical in nature. The knowledge and evidence generated through the process relating to practice should be used to improve learning and teaching. Transforming the knowledge and insights acquired through reflection into practical action is also a means of testing the theories of learning and teaching which the lecturer develops. Questions arise, such as:

- Does my practical theory about a teaching situation stand the test of being put into practice or do I have to modify, develop or change it?
- How can I develop strategies that fit my practical theories and are they likely to improve my teaching and the students' learning?
- How can I identify and select appropriate strategies from a range of alternatives available?
- How can I develop and put into place the strategies I want to try out?
- How can I monitor the effects of the strategies I have implemented and record their outcomes?

The above questions are generalised so that they can be used in any discipline area and teaching context. They are aimed at making the individual question their everyday practice in the learning environment. Developing one's own strategies is essential for good practice; however, the strategies must be underpinned by sound theory; one related to student learning or a specific pedagogic approach related to one's own discipline area.

Strategies also relate to planning, preparation and course design. Considerable discussion is given to areas such as session planning, aims and objectives, learning outcomes and evaluation. Despite the ILT making these areas of major concern, new lecturers should be concerned about them for the intrinsic value they hold to the craft of teaching and the effective learning of students. This book has attempted to direct the reader to what might constitute good practice. The issues and elements are not to be used as a template but more as a map that can give directions in which effective teaching and learning might develop. What constitutes good practice has been identified in each of the respective chapters. The elements of good practice may be placed under six generalised headings. These include:

1 Classroom teaching and learning

Good practice in classroom teaching requires a continuous awareness of:

- the students' prior knowledge;
- the students' prior conceptions of the subject area being taught;
- the students' present learning situation;
- the students' approaches to learning;
- the context in which you teach the students;
- the aims and learning outcomes for the particular session and the programme more generally;
- the need to evaluate and improve teaching.

Classroom teaching will improve if the above elements are kept in mind and continually improved. Student achievement is the essential element of success in the teaching situation.

2 Student learning

Student learning has been approached from a variety of perspectives in this book, suggesting that an understanding of the various theories and approaches is a good baseline from which to start understanding student learning. No one theory or perspective is given as a prescription for success; on the contrary, it is suggested that students operate differently in differing situations. However, there is evidence to show that students respond to the expectations of the lecturer. Hence, if memory and recall is required by the lecturer, students will respond at that level and are more likely to respond at a surface level rather than a deeper comprehension of the subject area that demands that students engage with the subject material through problem solving or discussion. Every teaching and learning experience is different. To encourage good practice the practitioner should gain an understanding of the principles of good teaching and learning, monitoring student achievement and the contexts in which students learn. This should include how students learn, what produces effective learning and how these elements can be reflected upon to further improve practice.

3 The teaching context

Teaching has often been referred to in this text. Contextual issues of teaching and learning can have a profound effect not only on those who are taught but on those who are doing the teaching. Key to the understanding of context is that what works with one group of students may not work with another. Flexibility is an important aspect to take account of when planning to teach the same topic to one or more groups of students. Sessions may be prepared for all groups, but the context in which they are taught will be significantly different; hence learning outcomes may well be different. Good practice suggests that flexibility and sensitivity on behalf of the lecturer are elements that make the difference between a good and a bad session. Learning your student group is the first step to success. The lecturer can create a context to teaching and learning to a certain degree; however, there are many elements that cannot be accounted for; hence the notion of flexibility and sensitivity to the students' learning needs is essential. Becoming more student focused and student centred may be a turning point in pedagogic practice.

4 Students' perceptions of teaching

When starting out in teaching it is easy to forget that students have conceptions of good and bad teaching and that it is the students who are the most important collaborators in the teaching and learning environment. The central focus of this book has been to make the lecturer aware of the need to understand the importance of student perception of teaching and the impact these perceptions have on learning outcomes. Good teaching requires the lecturer to understand his or her students and the expectations students have of the lecturer.

5 Student diversity

Increasingly in higher education student diversity has become a key issue. The student population is becoming more diverse, which in turn produces a more diverse teaching and learning situation as students come to a teaching session with widely different perspectives, knowledge base and cultural backgrounds. The implication for lecturers is that they need to become ever more aware of meeting the needs of all students they are responsible for.

Students from different cultures come with different expectations; some are more used to rote learning and others favour a more problem-solving approach to learning. Each student is entitled to learn. Prosser and Trigwell (1997, p. 170) suggest that:

> Good teachers will be monitoring the approaches and perceptions of all students. The processes of accommodating the variations in students' experiences also accommodate diversity, including cultural diversity. From our perspective, teaching with an awareness of cultural diversity is simply good teaching.

6 Reflection in and on practice

The final section in relation to good practice concerns the issues related to evaluation and monitoring of one's teaching. I have focused on evaluation relating primarily to reflection. This type of reflection considers the information gained or the evidence collected from evaluation, rather than the evaluation process itself. Reflection as discussed in Chapters 10 and 11 promotes active engagement with evidence as a means of promoting criticality and responsiveness to learning situations and development needs both of the lecturer and the student. Reflection is at the heart of effective teaching and learning.

Concluding comments

At the start of this book a context was set for the increased focus on teaching and learning in higher education. A brief description of the inception of the ILT was given to set the scene for areas of teaching and learning that have now become part of every new lecturer's induction into higher education. I conclude by referring to the elements of good practice that all academics should aim for if student achievement is to increase and teaching is to become more effective. The task is not a simple one but one that requires commitment to the process of continual improvement and an understanding of what it is to be involved in effective teaching and learning. It is hoped that this book will be a help to those who are starting out on this new journey.

Bibliography

Abercrombie, M. (1970) *Aims and Techniques of Group Teaching*. London: SRHE.

Abercrombie, M. (1993) *The Human Nature of Learning*: *Selections From the Work of M.L.J. Abercrombie*, ed. J.Nias. London: OU/SRHE.

Anderson, L.W. (ed.) (1984) *Time and School Learning*. London: Croom Helm.

Argyle, A. (1967) *The Psychology of Interpersonal Behaviour*. Harmondsworth: Penguin.

Ausubel, D.P., Novak, J.D. and Hanesian, H. (eds.) (1968) *Educational Psychology: A Cognitive View*. New York: Holt, Rinehart and Winston.

Barnes, D. (1987) *From Communication to Curriculum*. Harmondsworth: Penguin.

Barnett, R. (1996) Models of quality in teacher education. *Oxford Review of Education*, 22 (2), pp. 161–78.

Barnett, R. (1997) *Higher Education: A Critical Business*. Buckingham: SRHE/Open University Press.

Barris, R., Kielhofner, G. and Bauber, D. (1985) Educational experience and changes in learning and value preference. *Occupational Therapy Journal of Research*, 5, pp. 243–56.

Becher, T. (1989) *Academic Tribes and Territories*. Buckingham: SRHE/Open University Press.

Becher, T. (1996) The learning professions. *Studies in Higher Education*, 21 (1), pp. 43–56.

Berliner, D. (ed.) (1996) *Handbook of Educational Psychology*. New York: Macmillan.

Biggs, J. (1978) Individual and group differences in study processes. *British Journal of Educational Psychology*, 48, pp. 266–79.

Biggs, J. (1987) *Students' Approaches to Learning and Studying*. Hawthorn, Vic.: Australian Council for Educational Research.

Biggs, J. (1989) Approaches to the enhancement of tertiary teaching. *Higher Education Research and Development*, 8, pp. 7–25

Biggs, J. (1996) Enhancing teaching through constructive alignment. *Higher Education*, 32, pp. 1–18

Biggs, J. (1999) *Teaching for Quality Learning at University*. Buckingham: SRHE/Open University Press.

Bligh, D. (1986) *Teaching Thinking by Discussion*. Guildford: SRHE and NFER-Nelson.

Bligh, D. (1998) *What's the Use of Lecturers?* Harmondsworth: Penguin Books.

Bloom, B. (1964) *Taxonomy of Educational Objectives*, Vol. 1: *Cognitive Domain*. New York: McKay.

Bolam, R., Clark, J., Jones, K., Harper-Jones, G., Timbrell, T., Jones, R. and Thorpe, R. (1995) The induction of newly qualified teachers in schools: where next? *British Journal on In-service Education*, 21 (3).

Bork, A. (1987) Interaction: lessons from computer-based learning, in D. Laurillard (ed.) *Interactive Media: Working Methods and Practical Applications*. Chichester: Ellis Hortwood.

Boud, D. and Feletti, G. (1996) *The Challenge of Problem Based Learning*. London: Kogan Page.

Boud, D., Keogh, R. and Walker, D. (ed.) (1985) *Reflection: Turning Experience into Learning*. London: Kogan Page.

Bouffard,T., Boisvert, J., Vezeau, C. and Larouche, C. (1995) The impact of goal orientation on self-regulation and performance among college students. *British Journal of Educational Psychology*, 65, pp. 317–29.

Boyer, E. (1987) *College: The Undergraduate Experience in America*. New York: Harper Row.

Brew, A. and Wright, D. (1990) Changing teaching styles. *Distance Education*, 7 (2), pp. 183–212.

Brockbank, M. and McGill, J. (1998) *Facilitating Reflective Learning in Higher Education*. Buckingham: SRHE/Open University Press.

Brookfield, S.D. (1991) *Developing Critical Thinkers*. Milton Keynes: Open University Press.

Brophy, J. (1983) Research on the self-fulfilling prophecy and teacher expectations. *Journal of Educational Psychology*, 75 (5), pp. 631–61.

Brown, G. (1997) *Lecturing and Explaining*. London: Methuen

Brown, G. and Atkins, M. (1988) *Effective Teaching in Higher Education*. London: Methuen

Bruner, J.S. (1966) *Towards a Theory of Learning*. Cambridge, MA: Harvard University Press.

Burnard, P. (1995) *Learning Human Skills: An Experiential and Reflective Guide for Nurses* (3rd edn). Oxford: Butterworth/Heinemann, Jossey-Bass.

Butler, D.L. and Winne, P.H. (1995) Feedback and self-regulated learning: a theoretical synthesis. *Review of Educational Research*, 65 (3), pp. 245–81.

Candy, P.C. (1994) *Self-direction for Lifelong Learning: A Comprehensive Guide to Theory and Practice*. San Francisco: Jossey-Bass.

Canfield, A.A. (1976) *The Canfield Learning Styles Inventory*. Detroit: Humanics Media.

Carpenter, C.U. and Bruce, H. (1976) Competency based curriculum. The Kentucky model. *American Vocational Journal*, 52 (1), pp. 58–61

Claxton, G. (1984) *Live and Learn*. Milton Keynes: Open University Press.

Craft, A. (1996) *Professional Development*. Milton Keynes: Open University Press.

Darling. L. (2000) Portfolio as practice: the narratives of emerging teachers. *Teaching and Teacher Education*, 17 (1).

Dewey, J. (1933) *How we Think*. Chicago, IL: Regency.

Dunn, R., Deckinger, L., Withers, P. and Katzenstein, H. (1990) Should college students be taught how to do homework? *Illinois Research and Development Journal*, 26 (2), pp. 96–113.

Edgerton, R., Hutchings, P. and Quinlan, K. (1991) *The Teaching Portfolio: Capturing the Scholarship in Teaching.* Washington, DC: American Association of Higher Education.

Edwards, R. (1997) *Changing Places.* London: Routledge.

Entwistle, N. (1982) *Styles of Learning and Teaching*, London: John Wiley.

Entwistle, N. (1997) Introduction: phenomenography in higher education. *Higher Education*, 15, pp. 299–304.

Entwistle, N. and Marton, F. (1984) Changing conceptions of learning and research, in F. Marton (ed.) *The Experience of Learning.* Edinburgh: Scottish Academic Press.

Entwistle, N. and Ramsden, P. (1982) *Understanding Student Learning.* London: Croom Helm.

Eurat, M. (1985) Knowledge creation and knowledge use in professional contexts. *Studies in Higher Education*, 10 (2), pp. 117–33.

Eurat, M. (1994) *Developing Professional Knowledge and Competence.* London: Falmer Press.

Evans, G. (1991) Lessons in cognitive demands and student processing in upper secondary mathematics, in G. Evans (ed.) *Learning to Teach Cognitive Skills.* Melbourne: Australian Council for Educational Research.

Gagné, R.M. (1967) *The Conditions of Learning and Theory of Instruction* (1st edn). New York: Holt, Rinehart and Winston.

Gagné, R.M. (1985) *The Conditions of Learning and Theory of Instruction.* (4th edn). New York: Holt, Rinehart and Winston.

Gagné, R.M. and White, R. (1978) Memory structures and learning outcomes. *Review of Educational Research*, 48 (2), pp. 187–222.

Goldman, R. and Warren, R. (1972) Configuration in discriminant space: a heuristic approach to study techniques. Paper presented at the meeting of the Western Psychological Association, Portland.

Greeno, J.G. (1989) Situations, mental models and generative knowledge, in D. Klahr and K. Kotovsky (eds) *Complex Information Processing: The Impact of Herbet A. Simon.* Hillside, NJ: Erlbaum Associates.

Griffiths, S. and Partington, P. (1992) *Enabling Active Learning in Small Groups: Module 5 in Effective Learning and Teaching in Higher Education.* Sheffield: UCoSDA/CVCP.

Hatton, N. and Smith, D. (1995) Reflections in teacher education: towards definition and implementation. *Teacher and Teacher Education*, 7 (1), pp. 33–51.

Hayes, J. and Allinson, C.W. (1993) Matching learning styles and instructional strategy: an application of the person–environment interaction paradigm. *Perceptual and Motor Skills*, 76, pp. 63–79.

Hounsell, D.J. (1985) Learning and essay-writing. *Higher Education Research and Development*, 3, pp. 13–31.

Jones, G. (2000) *Leadership Training: The Most Vital Competency.* UCoSDA Conference. *http://www.shef.ac.uk/ucosda/pages/services/events.leadership.html*

Keefe, J.W. and Ferrell, B.G. (1990) Developing a defensible learning style paradigm. *Educational Leadership*, 48 (2), pp. 57–61.

Kibler, M. (1970) Behavioural objectives and speech – communication instruction. *Central States Speech Journal*, 21 (2), pp. 71–80.

Kolb, D. (1976) *Learning Styles Inventory* (Technical Manual). Boston, MA: McBar.

Kolb, D. (1984) *Experiential Learning: Experience as a source of Learning*. Englewood Cliffs, NJ: Prentice Hall.

Kotter, J.P. (1990) *A Force for Change: How Leadership Differs from Management*, New York: Free Press.

Layton, D. (ed.) (1963) *University Teaching in Transition*. London: Oliver & Boyd.

McGaghie, W. (1974) Learning in group settings: towards a classification of outcomes. *Educational Technology*, 14 (11), pp. 56–60.

MacIntyre, A. (1984) *After Virtue* (2nd edn). Notre Dame, IN: University of Notre Dame Press.

McKeachie, W.J., Pintrich, P.R., Lin, Y.G. and Smith, D.A.F. (1990) *Teaching and Learning in College Classrooms* (2nd edn). University of Michigan, National Center for Research to Improve Postsecondary Teaching and Learning.

Marton, F. (1976) What does it take to learn? Some implications of an alternative view of learning, in N.J. Entwistle (ed.) *Strategies for Research and Development in Higher Education*. Amsterdam: Swets and Zeitlinger.

Marton, F. (1988) Describing and improving learning, in R.R. Schmeck (ed.) *Learning Strategies and Learning Styles*. New York: Plenum.

Marton, F. and Saljo, R. (1976) On qualitative differences in learning: outcomes and process. *British Journal of Educational Psychology*, 46, pp. 4–11

Messick, S. (1984) The nature of cognitive styles: problems and promise in educational practice. *Educational Psychologist*, 19, pp. 59–74.

Mezirow, J. (1992) *Transformative Dimensions of Adult Learning*. San Francisco, CA: Jossey Bass.

NCIHE (1997) National Committee of Inquiry into Higher Education. Higher Education for a Learning Society. Dearing Report. London: HMSO.

Nicholls, G. (2001) *Professional Development in Higher Education: New Dimensions and Directions*. London: Kogan Page.

Pask, G. (1976) Styles and strategies of learning. *British Journal of Educational Psychology*, 46, pp. 128–48.

Peterson, P.L. and Walber, H.J. (eds) (1979) *Research on Teaching*. Berkeley, CA: McCutchan.

Prosser, M. (1994) A phenomenographic study of students' intuitive and conceptual understanding of certain electrical phenomena. *Instructional Science*, 22, pp. 189–205.

Prosser, M. and Trigwell, K. (1997) *Understanding Learning and Teaching: The Experience in Higher Education*. Buckingham: SRHE/Open University Press.

Ramsden, P. (1992). *Learning to Teach in Higher Education*. London: Routledge.

Ramsden, P. (1994) Describing and explaining research productivity. *Higher Education*, 27, pp. 207–26.

Ramsden, P. (1998) *Learning to Lead in Higher Education*. London: Routledge.

Reid, D.J. and Johnstone, M. (1999) Improving teaching in higher education: student and teacher perspectives. *Educational Studies*, 25 (3), pp. 269–81.

Riding, R. and Cheema, I. (1991) Cognitive styles – an overview and integration. *Educational Psychology*, 11 (3 and 4), pp. 193–215.

Robotham, D. (1999) *Application of Learning Style Theory in Higher Education*. http://www.chelt.ac.uk/el/philg/gdn/discuss/kolb2.htm

Rogers, C.R. (1969) *Freedom to Learn*. Cleveland, OH: Merrill.

Rogoff, B. (1990) *Apprenticeship in Thinking: Cognitive Development in Social Context*: New York: Oxford University Press.

Rowland, S. (1998) Turning academics into teachers? *Teaching in Higher Education*, 3 (2), pp. 303–14.

Ryles, G. (1944) *The Concept of Mind*. London: Hutchinson.

Saljo, R. (1982) *Learning and Understanding: A Study of Differences in Constructing Meaning From a Text*. Gothenburg: Acta Universitatis Gothenburgensis.

Schon, D. (1988) *The Reflective Practitioner*. London: Temple Smith.

Schmeck, R.R. (1983) Learning styles of college students, in R.F. Dillon and R.R. Schmeck (eds) *Individual Differences in Cognition. Vol. 1*. New York: Academic Press.

Seldin, P. (1991) *The Teaching Portfolio. A Practical Guide to Improved Performance and Promotions*. Bolton, MA: Anker.

Shulman, L. (1987) Knowledge and teaching: foundations of the new reform. *Harvard Educational Review*, 57 (1), pp. 1–22.

Siedentop, D. (1991) *Developing Teaching Skills in Physical Education*. London: Mayfield Press.

Standing, T. and Shevels, T. (1994) The management of learning groups – empirical evidence. *Training and Management Development Methods*, 8 (5), pp. 5–10.

Stenhouse, L. (1972) Teaching through small group discussion: formality, rules and authority, in C.F. Page and H. Greenway (eds) *Innovation in Higher Education*. London: SRHE.

Streufert, S. and Nogami, G.Y. (1989) Cognitive styles and complexity: implications for industrial and organisational psychology, in C.L. Cooper and I. Robertson (eds) *International Review of Industrial and Organisational Psychology*. Chichester: Wiley.

Svensson, L. (1977) On qualitative differences in learning III – study skills and learning. *British Journal of Educational Psychology*, 47, pp. 233–43.

Talbot, R. (1985) Situational influences on learning styles. *Industrial and Commercial Training*, 23 (1), pp. 19–28.

Taylor, K.L. (1993) The role of scholarship in university teaching. *Canadian Journal of Higher Education*, 23 (3), pp. 64–79.

Thomas, P.R. and Bain, J.D. (1984) Contextual dependence of learning approaches: the effects of assessment. *Human Learning*, 3, pp. 227–40.

Trigwell, K.T. and Prosser, M. (1990) Using student learning outcomes measures in the evalution of teaching. *Research and Development in Higher Education*, 13, pp. 390–7.

Walker, M. (1994) Students' plagiarism in universities – what are we doing about it? *Higher Education Research and Development*, 17, pp. 89–106.

Winsor P., Butt, R.L. and Reeves, H. (1999) Portraying professional development in preservice teacher education. *Teachers and Teaching*, 5 (1), pp. 33–59.

Witkin, H.A. (1977) Field-dependent and field-independent cognitive styles and their educational implications. *Review of Educational Research*, 47 (1), pp. 1–64.

Wittrock, M. (1986) Students' thought processes, in M. Wittrock (ed.) *Handbook of Research on Teaching*. New York: Macmillan.

Wolfe, D.M and Kolb, D. (1984) Career development, personal growth and experiential learning in organisational psychology, in D. Kolb, I. Rubin and J. McIntyre (eds) *Readings on Human Behaviour*, 4th edn. New Jersey: Prentice Hall.

Index